D1662625

STARK

TRAINING
QUALI 2013

Englisch
Bayern
2007–2012

STARK

Umschlagbild: © Grant Berkeley/www.sxc.hu

ISBN 978-3-8490-0193-3

© 2012 by Stark Verlagsgesellschaft mbH & Co. KG
7. ergänzte Auflage
www.stark-verlag.de

Inhalt

Autorin: Birgit Mohr

Vorwort

Liebe Schülerin, lieber Schüler,

dieses Buch ist das Lösungsheft zu dem Band **Training Quali Englisch Bayern** (Titel-Nummer 93555). Es enthält ausführliche kommentierte Lösungsvorschläge zu den Übungsaufgaben.

Diese Lösungsvorschläge ermöglichen es dir, deine Leistung einzuschätzen. Durch die **Tipps und Hinweise** zu den einzelnen Aufgaben lernst du, was bei einer bestimmten Aufgabenstellung von dir erwartet wird.

Viel Erfolg im Quali wünscht dir

Birgit Mohr

Allgemeiner Hinweis: Zum Lösen aller folgenden Aufgaben zum Kapitel „Listening" musst du dir den Text genau anhören. Wenn du ihn nach dem ersten Hören noch nicht verstanden hast, kannst du ihn dir natürlich auch öfter anhören. Lies dir den Hörverstehenstext nur durch, wenn du mit den Lösungen ganz unsicher bist und gar nicht weiterkommst.

Listening Comprehension Test 1: In the supermarket

1 Dear customers, welcome to Richie's Supermarket, where you can always get a bargain!
This week we are celebrating health week at Richie's Supermarket, and we take special care to offer you the best products for the health of your whole family at
5 the best prices you can find!
In our fruit and vegetable department, you can pick your choice of the best apples, pears or tomatoes for just 59 pence per kilo! Yes, that's one kilo of apples, pears or tomatoes for just 59 pence! By the way, the 5 kilogram bag of potatoes now costs only 1 pound 79.
10 Or, if you are looking for some relaxing moments, why don't you visit our cosmetics department, where you will find a wide selection of natural bath products for just 99 pence each. Imagine, you can take a refreshing, relaxing bath, with the fragrance of your choice, for just 99 pence! What's more, all sun lotions are now reduced by 25 %.
15 Dear customers, at Richie's Supermarket we care for your health. Take your time to find out about our offers, and enjoy your health week with us!

Aufgabe 1

a) Richie's
Hinweis: Z. 1

b) health week
Hinweis: Z. 3

Aufgabe 2

a) 59 pence
Hinweis: Z. 6 f.

1

b) 1 pound 79 pence
  / Hinweis: *Z. 8 f.*

c) 99 pence
  / Hinweis: *Z. 11 f.*

d) 25 %
  / Hinweis: *Z. 13 f.*

Aufgabe 3

a) *wrong:* protests, *correct:* products

b) *wrong:* friend, *correct:* fruit

c) *wrong:* normal, *correct:* natural

d) *wrong:* money, *correct:* time

Listening Comprehension Test 2: At the airport

Part 1: At the check-in

(Busy sound of airport in the background, flight announcements.)

MR MILLER *(out of breath):* Good afternoon, my wife and I have tickets to Munich.
I hope we are not too late for the flight.

5 WOMAN AT SERVICE DESK: Please give me your tickets and your passports.

MR MILLER: Here you are.

WOMAN AT SERVICE DESK: Thank you. OK, let me check, Mr and Mrs Miller.

(Sound of typing on a computer keyboard in the background, more airport sounds.)

WOMAN AT SERVICE DESK: Mr and Mrs Miller, you are going to Munich via
10 Frankfurt?

MR MILLER: Yes, we have to change planes in Frankfurt.

(More typing on a computer keyboard in the background.)

WOMAN AT SERVICE DESK: OK, you are still on time for the flight to Frankfurt. But
you have to hurry – the plane is going to take off in 20 minutes! Where would
15 you like to sit in the plane, by the window or on the aisle?

MR MILLER: On the aisle, please.

WOMAN AT SERVICE DESK: No problem. I am giving you two seats in the centre
row – one of them is next to the aisle. Would you like to check in any luggage?

MR MILLER: No, thanks, we have only hand luggage.

20 WOMAN AT SERVICE DESK: OK.

(More typing on a computer keyboard in the background.)

Woman at service desk: Here are your boarding cards to Frankfurt, and from Frankfurt to Munich. Please proceed to Gate 17 immediately.
Mr Miller: Thank you!
25 Woman at service desk: Enjoy your flight!

Aufgabe 1

a) right
  Hinweis: Z. 3

b) false
  Hinweis: Z. 5 f.

c) false
  Hinweis: Z. 16

d) false
  Hinweis: Z. 19

Aufgabe 2

a) their tickets and passports
  Hinweis: Z. 5

b) Frankfurt
  Hinweis: Z. 10 f.

c) in 20 minutes
  Hinweis: Z. 14

d) 17
  Hinweis: Z. 23

Part 2: Boarding the plane

(Busy sounds of passengers boarding the airplane, indistinguishable talking and laughter in the background.)
Woman: Excuse me, sir?
5 Mr Miller *(startled)*: Who? Me?
Woman: Yes, sir. Excuse me, I'm sorry to bother you but it looks like you are sitting in my seat.
Mr Miller: Oh, really? Let me check our boarding cards …
(Sound of rustling in a travel bag.)
10 Mr Miller: Hmm, where are they … just a moment.
Woman: Sure, no hurry.
(More sound of rustling in a travel bag.)

3

MR MILLER: Ah, here they are. Let me just check ... Here, please take a look, my wife and I have seats 21D and 21E. Which seat do you have?

15 WOMAN: Oops, that's strange. My seat number is 21E, too!

MR MILLER: This is very strange. It must be the airline's mistake!

WOMAN *(sighing)*: It must be! Wait a moment, I'm just going to ask the flight attendant.

(Some time passes. More sounds of passengers boarding the airplane in the back-
20 *ground.)*

FLIGHT ATTENDANT: Hello, sir! This lady tells me that you have the same seat as she does. Could you please show me your boarding cards?

MR MILLER: Yes, of course. Here, these are the boarding cards for my wife and myself.

25 FLIGHT ATTENDANT *(reads aloud)*: 21D and 21E ... Mr and Mrs Miller ... The flight number and date are correct. You really are sitting in the right seat. Ma'am, could you show me your boarding card again, please?

WOMAN *(irritated)*: OK, here it is.

FLIGHT ATTENDANT: Ah, that's it! Ma'am, this boarding card is for another flight.
30 Look, it has the same flight number, but the date was two weeks ago! Did you travel to Frankfurt two weeks ago, too?

WOMAN *(embarrassed)*: Oh, yes, you're right, excuse me. This is my fault, it's the wrong boarding card. I travel to Frankfurt every two weeks and that's an old one. Let me just check in my bag ...

35 FLIGHT ATTENDANT: No problem for you, Mr and Mrs Miller, you have the right seats.

MR MILLER: OK, thank you.

WOMAN: I'm afraid I can't find my boarding card, I don't know where I put it.

FLIGHT ATTENDANT: That's no problem. Please come with me and I will look up
40 your seat on the computer. *(Voice fading)* It's not the first time that somebody lost their boarding card on the way from the gate to the plane ...

Aufgabe 3

a) B
   Hinweis: Z. 6 f.

b) A
   Hinweis: Z. 16

c) C
   Hinweis: Z. 25 f.

d) C
/ Hinweis: *Z. 29*
e) B
/ Hinweis: *Z. 38*

Aufgabe 4

a) 21E
b) boarding card
c) 2 weeks before
d) computer

Listening Comprehension Test 3: Mrs Brown at the shoe store

Part 1

SHOP ASSISTANT: Hello, how can I help you?
MRS BROWN: Hello, I'm looking for a pair of shoes for the summer.
SHOP ASSISTANT: Do you have something specific in mind?
5 MRS BROWN *(hesitantly)*: Mm, yes. I'd like a pair of comfortable leather shoes.
SHOP ASSISTANT: What colour are you looking for?
MRS BROWN: A light colour please, maybe white or beige.
SHOP ASSISTANT: OK, please come over to our summer section.

Aufgabe 1

a) summer
/ Hinweis: *Z. 3*
b) comfortable
/ Hinweis: *Z. 5*
c) beige or white
/ Hinweis: *Z. 7*

Part 2

SHOP ASSISTANT: Here, take a look at this pair. They are a new design from Italy
and are very comfortable. Are these the type of shoes you like to wear?
MRS BROWN: Not exactly. These shoes are too high – I don't think I could wear
5 them for more than an hour. I also don't like it that my toes show. I'd like a
closed pair of shoes that I can wear with socks.

SHOP ASSISTANT: Of course. Please come over to this aisle, where we have the more casual shoes.

SHOP ASSISTANT *(after a moment)*: Here, please have a look. What do you think of these loafers, which are a nice beige? These are from another collection from Italy.

MRS BROWN: Oh, yes, they do look nice! I think I'd like to try them.

SHOP ASSISTANT: What size can I get for you?

MRS BROWN: That would be a 5, thank you.

Aufgabe 2

a) toes
   Hinweis: Z. 5

b) socks
   Hinweis: Z. 6

c) Italy
   Hinweis: Z. 10 ff.

Part 3

SHOP ASSISTANT: How do the shoes fit? Do they feel comfortable?

MRS BROWN: Phew, I'm afraid they don't fit. Have you got them half a size larger?

SHOP ASSISTANT: One moment, I'll go to the back again to look. I'm not sure that we still have this style in 5 ½, I think we've already sold all of them. *(pause while he goes to look)*

MRS BROWN *(full of expectation)*: And, have you got them in 5 ½?

SHOP ASSISTANT: Sorry, I'm afraid not. Size 5 ½ is completely sold out. But I did bring you a size 6. Would you like to have a try?

MRS BROWN: Oh, that's a pity ... but OK, I'll try them.

MRS BROWN *(after a moment)*: Let's see ...

SHOP ASSISTANT: What do you think, do they fit nicely?

MRS BROWN *(hesitantly)*: Yes, I think they do fit! But I'm a bit surprised that I'm a size 6 now!

SHOP ASSISTANT: Don't worry, this make is sometimes a bit tighter than others.

MRS BROWN: OK. *(After a moment)* Well, I've made up my mind – I would like to buy these shoes.

SHOP ASSISTANT: Perfect!

Aufgabe 3

a) fit
   Hinweis: Z. 3

b) 5.5
   Hinweis: Z. 3 *ff.*

c) 6
   Hinweis: Z. 14 *ff.*

Part 4

(sound of electronic cash register)

GIRL AT CASH REGISTER *(cordially)*: Hello, how are you today? What would you like to pay for?

5 MRS BROWN: That pair of beige loafers, please.

GIRL AT CASH REGISTER: OK.

GIRL AT CASH REGISTER *(over the sound of electronic cash register)*: That'll be forty-nine ninety-five. Would you like to pay by cash or credit card?

MRS BROWN: I'd like to pay by credit card, please. Here you are.

10 GIRL AT CASH REGISTER: Thanks!

GIRL AT CASH REGISTER *(after a moment)*: So, here are your shoes. Thanks very much. Goodbye now.

MRS BROWN: Thanks. Goodbye!

Aufgabe 4

a) true
   Hinweis: Z. 5

b) false
   Hinweis: Z. 7 *f.*

c) true
   Hinweis: Z. 9

Aufgabe 1

a) At school you find chalk, <u>a blackboard</u> and <u>pupils</u> for example.

b) In winter when it is cold there is <u>snow</u> and <u>ice</u>.

c) In the zoo there are a lot of animals, for example a monkey, <u>a tiger</u> and <u>a bear</u>.

Aufgabe 2

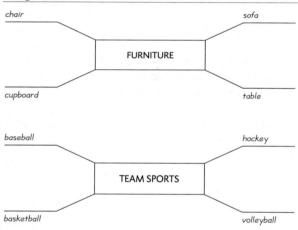

Aufgabe 3

Hinweis: *In dieser Aufgabe ist der Oberbegriff nicht vorgegeben. Du musst überlegen, was die aufgelisteten Wörter gemeinsam haben.*

a) colours

b) musical instruments

c) nationalities

Aufgabe 4

Hinweis: *Zu Beginn jeder Zeile ist der Oberbegriff vorgegeben. Du musst also nur noch überlegen, welches Wort nicht dazu passt.*

a) pineapple
   Hinweis: *kein Gemüse*

b) Texas
   Hinweis: *kein Land*

c) vinegar
   Hinweis: *kein Getränk*

d) fork
   Hinweis: *keine Mahlzeit*

e) Democratic
   Hinweis: *keine Religion*

Aufgabe 5

Hinweis: *Hier musst du überlegen, welches Wort nicht in die Reihe passt und was die verbliebenen Wörter gemeinsam haben.*

a) ~~bag~~ → clothes
   Hinweis: *„bag" ist kein Kleidungsstück, „clothes" ist das* **collective noun**

b) ~~pen~~ → car
   Hinweis: *„pen" ist kein Teil eines Autos, „car" ist das* **collective noun**

c) ~~food~~ → parts of the body
   Hinweis: *„food" ist kein Körperteil, „parts of the body" ist das* **collective noun**

d) ~~knife~~ → vegetables
   Hinweis: *„knife" ist kein Gemüse, „vegetables" ist das* **collective noun**

e) ~~meat~~ → desserts
   Hinweis: *„meat" ist kein Nachtisch, „dessert" ist das* **collective noun**

Aufgabe 6

a) restaurant
b) theatre
c) hospital
d) church

e) gym

f) park

Aufgabe 7

would – wood
board – bored
whole – hole
know – no
break – brake
hour – our
piece – peace
see – sea

Aufgabe 8

✎ **Hinweis:** *Wenn dir einige englische Begriffe für das Land, die Sprache oder die Nationalität nicht auf Anhieb einfallen, schlage sie nach und lerne die Vokabeln.*

a) Big Ben is a tourist attraction in London. London is in England and people there speak <u>English</u>.

b) In Amsterdam you will find the "Anne Frank House". That is in the Netherlands. The people there are called the <u>Dutch</u>.

c) The Beyazit Tower is a symbol of Istanbul. Istanbul is in Turkey and people there speak <u>Turkish</u>.

d) The Leaning Tower of Pisa is in Italy. The people there speak <u>Italian</u>.

e) The famous Eiffel Tower is in Paris. The people there are French. Most people in <u>France</u> only speak <u>French</u>.

f) The Puerta del Sol is in Madrid. This is in Spain. The people who live in Madrid are <u>Spanish</u>.

Aufgabe 9

✎ **Hinweis:** *Hier sollst du die Gegenteile der aufgelisteten Begriffe aufführen. Nicht nur zu Adjektiven wie „hell" gibt es ein Gegenteil („dunkel"), sondern auch zu Verben kann ein Gegenteil gefunden werden.*

a) It was <u>light</u> this morning when I went to school.

b) The plane was <u>early</u> this morning.

c) I often <u>catch</u> the train.

d) Where can I <u>sell</u> a watch, please?

e) The classroom is <u>empty</u>.

Aufgabe 10

a) ugly

b) wet

c) sell

d) low

e) wide

f) sunny

g) start

h) clean

Aufgabe 11

a) hot

b) day

c) down

d) fast

e) asleep

f) sad

Aufgabe 12

a) daughter

b) queen

c) sister

d) waitress

Aufgabe 13

Hinweis: *Zur Kontrolle, ob du die Lücken korrekt ausgefüllt hast, kannst du dir am Ende den gesamten Text noch einmal durchlesen. Wenn du bemerkst, dass manche Sätze keinen Sinn ergeben, musst du dir andere Lösungsmöglichkeiten überlegen.*

a) CLARA: Hi Eric, how <u>are</u> you?

b) ERIC: <u>Fine</u>, thanks. How are you?

c) CLARA: I'm fine, too. But I <u>miss</u> you all.

d) ERIC: We <u>miss</u> you, <u>too</u>. <u>When</u> are you coming home?

e) CLARA: <u>On</u> Friday.

f) ERIC: We're looking forward <u>to</u> seeing you.

Aufgabe 14

a) Where are you / do you come from?

b) When is your birthday?

c) What's your favourite colour?

d) Do you have / Have you got any brothers and sisters?

e) Do you have / Have you got any pets?

Aufgabe 15

a) Where are you from? / Where do you live?

b) How old are you?

c) Why are you here?

d) Do you like it here?

e) Have you ever been here before?

Aufgabe 16

a) I would like a loaf of bread, please.

b) Could you tell me the way to the next bus station?

c) I'd like to have the menu, please.

d) Do you have this pair of jeans one size bigger?

Aufgabe 17

a) Does this train go to the airport?

b) Do you sell stamps?

c) Please give me the map.

d) I'd like to have chocolate ice-cream.

Aufgabe 18

Hinweis: *Die Antworten geben dir Aufschluss darüber, welches Fragewort du verwenden musst.*

a) <u>Where</u> is the cafeteria?

b) <u>How much</u> is a sandwich?

c) <u>Who</u> is that girl over there?

d) <u>Why</u> is she looking so sad?

e) <u>When</u> did she move?

Aufgabe 19

SARA: "Lisa and I are going <u>to come</u> to Paris on 12th May."

PIERRE: "When <u>will</u> you arrive in Paris?"

SARA: "At 2.35 p.m."

PIERRE: "<u>What</u> is the name of the hotel you're staying at?"

SARA: "<u>It's</u> Park Hotel."

PIERRE: "Do you have any <u>plans</u> for your stay?"

SARA: "I want to do some <u>shopping/sightseeing</u> and visit the Eiffel Tower and the Champs-Elysées."

PIERRE: "I would like <u>to show you</u> the nightlife in Paris. I'm looking <u>forward</u> to seeing you next <u>week</u>."

Aufgabe 20

a) railway station

b) travel agency

c) a suitcase

d) passport

Aufgabe 21

a) newspaper

b) a pen

c) a mobile phone

d) a key

Aufgabe 22

Hinweis: Hier musst du nicht auf die Verwendung der richtigen Zeit achten, sondern ausschließlich darauf, dass du das richtige Verb einsetzt.

"I'm going to <u>wear</u> my suit and I <u>think</u> I will be very nervous. I <u>hope</u> I won't <u>forget</u> my lines. Even my grandparents <u>want</u> to come and <u>see</u> me acting. I hope everyone will <u>enjoy</u> the evening."

Aufgabe 23

Hinweis: Für die Verwendung der Präpositionen gibt es keine feste Regel. Am besten lernst du die jeweiligen Präpositionen gleich zusammen mit den entsprechenden Verben. In der Grammatik findest du ab Seite 85 eine Übersicht über wichtige Präpositionen im Englischen.

a) The teacher is sitting <u>at</u> the table.

b) John has never been <u>to</u> the United States.

c) What do you think <u>of/about</u> bungee jumping?

d) The new girl is <u>from</u> Brighton.

e) I am waiting <u>for</u> you at the station.

Aufgabe 24

Hinweis: Es ist wichtig, dass du die Wörter mit unregelmäßigen Pluralformen auswendig lernst.

a) knives

b) mice

c) men

d) women

e) children

f) fish

g) leaves

h) teeth

Aufgabe 25

Hinweis: *In den folgenden Aufgaben musst du bestimmte Wendungen aus dem Deutschen ins Englische übertragen. Überlege genau, wie die korrekte englische Formulierung lautet. Versuche, nicht Wort für Wort aus dem Deutschen zu übersetzen.*

a) I don't like Brad Pitt's new film/movie;

I don't like the new film with Brad Pitt.

b) Can I have/I'd like/I'll have a coke and (a piece of) cake, please?

c) Please don't smoke./Would you mind not smoking?

d) What do you think of/about piercings?

e) How/What about watching a film/video?/Why don't we watch a film/video?

f) I don't want to/I'm not going to/I don't intend to/I won't spend much/a lot of/a large amount of money at the weekend.

Aufgabe 26

a) DVDs are more expensive than videos.

b) Where can I/you buy/get the best ice-cream in town?

c) Don't mention it./You're welcome./Not at all.

Aufgabe 27

a) That's okay./I don't mind.

b) Sorry, (but) I'm very/so busy at the moment./now.

c) Have a nice holiday./Have a good time./Enjoy your holiday.

d) Are you interested in tennis?

Aufgabe 28

a) Excuse me, could you tell me the way to/do you know the way to/can you tell me the way to the Statue of Liberty, please?

b) Sorry,/Pardon, I didn't understand/get you.

c) Excuse me, is there anybody sitting here?/can I sit here?/is this seat taken/free?/do you mind if I sit here?

d) I'm going back to Germany by plane tonight/this evening.

e) Have you ever been to Germany?

f) What a pity/It's a shame that the weather is so bad./I wish the weather weren't so bad.

Aufgabe 29

Hinweis: Beachte bei der Umformung in verneinte Sätze auch die Zeitform! Die Regeln, wie du in den verschiedenen Zeiten die Verneinungsform bildest, findest du auf Seite 90 ff.

a) The sun isn't shining outside.

b) Jill doesn't want to buy a new pullover.

c) Mr Weaver didn't enjoy the film he watched yesterday.

d) Jack won't visit his grandparents in Dover this summer.

e) The Smiths don't have a new car.

f) Sara doesn't have a dog.

g) It is not/isn't going to rain tomorrow.

h) The summer holidays won't last longer this year.

i) I didn't do all my homework on Friday.

j) They aren't travelling around Europe.

k) Lucy doesn't like going to the cinema.

Aufgabe 30

*Hinweis: Die Regeln zur **word order** im Englischen kannst du auf Seite 90 in der Grammatik nachlesen.*

a) Pete is going to visit his aunt and uncle in California.

b) They invited him to spend the summer with them.

c) Mary is jealous that her brother is going to make a trip.

d) Mary's aunt promises that she can visit them soon, too.

Aufgabe 31

Hinweis: *Die Regeln zur Verwendung des* **present progressive** *findest du auf Seite 91 in der Grammatik.*

a) What are you <u>doing</u> in this picture?

b) I <u>am carrying</u> a large watermelon I bought at the market.

c) Look, the dress I <u>am wearing</u> in this picture is new.

d) The sun <u>is shining</u> in every picture.

e) Here we <u>are going</u> down to the beach.

Aufgabe 32

Hinweis: *Die Regeln zur Verwendung des* **going-to-future** *kannst du in der Grammatik auf Seite 94 nachlesen.*

a) I <u>am going to meet</u> Jane on Saturday for breakfast.

b) On Monday I <u>am going to see</u> the doctor.

c) I <u>am going to go</u> camping with some of my friends.

Aufgabe 33

Hinweis: *Die Regeln zum* **simple past** *kannst du noch einmal ab Seite 92 der Grammatik nachlesen.*

On Saturday morning Kelly and Sara <u>met</u> in town to do some shopping. They <u>were</u> invited to a birthday party in the evening and <u>wanted</u> to buy a present. At first they <u>couldn't</u> really decide what to buy, but then they <u>saw</u> the new Eminem CD and <u>were</u> sure that that would be the right present for Tim. Now they <u>could</u> take a look around for some cheap and trendy clothes for the party. Kelly <u>bought</u> a new T-shirt, but Sara <u>didn't</u> find anything. Afterwards they <u>went</u> home to get changed for the party.

Aufgabe 34

Hinweis: *Hier musst du entscheiden, welche Zeitform korrekt ist. Signalwörter wie yesterday, now, last week, etc. helfen dir dabei, die richtige Zeit anzuwenden. Du kannst dazu noch einmal alle Regeln in der Grammatik ab Seite 90 nachlesen.*

a) I <u>felt</u> very sick yesterday. Then I went to bed early and now <u>I'm feeling</u>/<u>I feel</u> much better.

b) In 1982, my brother <u>was</u> born.

c) I <u>am going to move</u>/<u>I'm moving</u> to Australia in October. I can't stand the English weather any longer.

d) My aunt <u>gave</u> me this book for my birthday last week.

Aufgabe 35

a) <u>Do you have</u> the latest Maroon 5 CD?

b) No, I'm sorry. We <u>ran</u> out yesterday. At the moment we <u>are waiting</u> for the new delivery.

c) <u>Do you sell</u> concert tickets? I'm interested in the open air festival that <u>will take place</u> in summer.

d) Yes, of course we <u>sell</u> tickets for the festival. But you will have to come back in 2 weeks to buy a ticket.

Aufgabe 36

1	2	3	4
C	A	D	B

Aufgabe 37

Hinweis: *Adverbien beschreiben unter anderem, auf welche Art etwas geschieht.*

a) gladly

b) easily

c) well

d) closely

Aufgabe 38

Hinweis: *Die Signalwörter für die Verwendung des* **simple present** *findest du auf Seite 91 in der Grammatik. Beachte bei der Bildung des* **simple present** *den Merksatz: „He, she, it – ,s' muss mit!"*

a) Mum <u>always</u> **wakes** me up in the morning.

b) Sally <u>often</u> **goes** hiking at the weekends.

c) Normally Mr Jones **spends** his holidays in Ireland.

d) <u>On Mondays</u>, Jane **is** late for school. The rest of the week she <u>usually</u> **arrives** on time.

e) Lisa <u>never</u> **does** her homework properly.

Aufgabe 39

Hinweis: *Die Regeln zur Steigerung von Adjektiven findest du auf Seite 88 f. der Grammatik.*

a) Jill is <u>taller</u> than Jenny.

b) Jim is <u>the tallest</u> boy in our class.

c) Sara has <u>the longest</u> hair.

d) Michelle's hair is <u>darker</u> than Tina's.

e) Toby is <u>better</u> at playing football than Mark.

f) But Lisa plays <u>(the) best</u>!

Aufgabe 40

a) This year the weather was much <u>better</u> than last year. The sun was shining almost every day.

b) Our flat was not <u>as comfortable as</u> last year: the furniture was a bit old.

c) The only thing I did not enjoy was the food: in a foreign country you always get <u>worse</u> bread than in Germany.

d) The people in Spain are a lot <u>nicer</u> than people at home: they are very interested in foreign people and want to know everything about our lives.

e) My uncle has been thinking about moving to Spain for years because he thinks everything is <u>better</u> there."

f) We went to Italy. The weather wasn't <u>as good as</u> in Spain. It was raining most of the time.

g) I went there with a youth group because that way I thought it would be <u>more exciting than</u> spending the holidays with my parents in Wales, like I did for the last five years.

h) In my opinion, Italian food is the <u>best</u> in Europe.

i) That was the best holiday I've ever had and being back here is even <u>worse</u> than the rain in Italy."

Aufgabe 41

Hinweis: Hier musst du die fehlenden **pronouns** *(Fürwörter) einsetzen. Die Regeln zur Verwendung von* **pronouns** *findest du auf Seite 79 der Grammatik.*

Mrs Brown comes into the classroom, looks out of the window and asks her class in surprise, "Whose jacket is that lying outside?" John answers, "<u>It</u> is Lisa's." "Lisa, is that true? Is that y<u>our</u> jacket?" Mrs Brown asks. "Go and get <u>it</u>, please." Then Mrs Brown notices that Lisa is not in the classroom. "Where is <u>she</u> today?" "<u>I</u> think <u>she</u> is ill," says Maggie, who sounds as if she has been crying, "<u>She</u> didn't wait for <u>me</u> this morning like <u>she</u> usually does. <u>I</u> borrowed <u>her</u> jacket yesterday and <u>she</u> told me to look after <u>it</u>. But this morning, Jack and Tim took the jacket and threw <u>it</u> around. <u>I</u> couldn't catch <u>it</u>, and then <u>they</u> threw <u>it</u> out of the window." "Is that true, y<u>ou</u> two?" asks Mrs Brown, "Did y<u>ou</u> do that? Go and get the jacket immediately, give <u>it</u> back to Maggie and say sorry to <u>her</u>. <u>You</u> will stay behind after school and clean up the classroom." Jack is very angry and says, "<u>It</u> wasn't <u>me</u>!" <u>He</u> points at Tim: "<u>He</u> did it – <u>it</u> was all <u>his</u> fault!" Mrs Brown turns to the whole class and says, "All of y<u>ou</u> saw <u>them</u> take the jacket and throw <u>it</u> out of the window, and did any of y<u>ou</u> help Maggie? No, y<u>ou</u> didn't. <u>I</u> have decided that y<u>ou</u> will all stay behind after school and clean up the classroom. Maggie, y<u>ou</u> go to Lisa's house straight after school, return the jacket to <u>her</u> and explain what <u>we/they</u> did at school today. And now, everyone, please show <u>me</u> y<u>our</u> homework!"

Aufgabe 42

Hinweis: Die Regeln zu den **relative clauses** *und zur Verwendung der* **relative pronouns** *kannst du in der Grammatik auf Seite 87 f. nachlesen.*

a) Doesn't the pullover <u>which</u>/<u>that</u> is lying on the floor belong to you?

b) The man <u>who</u> lives next door had an accident yesterday.

c) I can't find the book <u>which</u>/<u>that</u> you lent me last week.

d) The woman <u>who</u> is sitting next to you is my mother.

e) The train <u>which</u>/<u>that</u> arrived late was very crowded.

Aufgabe 43

Hinweis: *Die Regeln zu den* **if-clauses** *kannst du in der Grammatik auf den Seiten 78 f. nachlesen.*

a) If I take the train, I <u>will be</u> late.

b) If you don't take an umbrella with you, you <u>will get</u> wet.

c) If I move to America, I <u>will improve</u> my English.

d) If you <u>are</u> afraid to fly, it is better to travel by car.

e) If I <u>buy</u> the house, I will pay no rent.

Allgemeiner Hinweis: In diesem Kapitel wird dein Leseverständnis überprüft. Da du hier die Möglichkeit hast, dir den Text noch einmal durchzulesen, werden genauere Details abgefragt als in den Aufgaben zum Hörverstehen. Du solltest die Texte also besonders aufmerksam lesen.

Reading Comprehension Test 1: London attractions

Aufgabe 1

Hinweis: Bei dieser Aufgabe sollst du jeder Person bzw. Personengruppe jeweils eine Londoner Sehenswürdigkeit zuordnen. Hier ist es hilfreich, wenn du dir überlegst, was die einzelnen Personen auszeichnet und welche Sehenswürdigkeit am besten zu diesen Merkmalen passt.

London Planetarium: b

Phantom of the Opera: d

Tate Modern: a

Legoland Windsor: c

Aufgabe 2

Hinweis: Auch hier sollst du wieder zuordnen. Jetzt musst du dir überlegen, welches Foto zu welcher Sehenswürdigkeit passt. Vielleicht hilft es dir, wenn du dir die Texte zu den Sehenswürdigkeiten noch einmal durchliest.

The London Planetarium	Phantom of the Opera	Tate Modern	Legoland Windsor
6	4	2	5

Aufgabe 3

Hinweis: Hier musst du erkennen, welches Wort in dem Satz falsch ist. Die entsprechenden Informationen dazu findest du im Lesetext. Das falsche Wort streichst du durch und schreibst den kompletten, korrigierten Satz auf.

a) In "The London Planetarium" you can watch shows about <u>stars</u>.

b) The musical „Phantom of the Opera" is based upon a <u>novel</u> about the singer Christine and the mysterious masked man.

c) In "Tate Modern" pieces of art are exhibited from <u>1900</u> to the present day.

d) "Legoland Windsor" offers a lot of detailed <u>reproductions</u>.

Aufgabe 4

Hinweis: *Alle Informationen, die du zum Beantworten dieser Fragen brauchst, findest du in den Texten zu den einzelnen Sehenswürdigkeiten.*

a) One show lasts 10–12 minutes.
   Hinweis: *siehe Annonce 1*

b) Digistar 2 is the most advanced projector in the world. That is what makes the "London Planetarium" unique.
   Hinweis: *siehe Annonce 1*

c) In Tate Modern you can find pictures from 1900 up to the present day.
   Hinweis: *siehe Annonce 2*

d) Michael Crawford played the leading role in the premiere of "The Phantom of the Opera" in London.
   Hinweis: *siehe Annonce 3*

e) The main attraction of "Legoland Windsor" is the reproduction of cities with people and landscape.
   Hinweis: *siehe Annonce 4*

Reading Comprehension Test 2: Cinema

Aufgabe 1

Hinweis: *In dieser Aufgabe musst du die Bedürfnisse und Wünsche der Zuschauer genau erkennen und ihnen dann den passenden Film zuordnen. Dabei hilft es, wenn du dir die Werbung des Kinos noch einmal sorgfältig durchliest.*

a) D – Lord of the Rings
   Hinweis: Lord of the Rings ist ein Fantasyfilm.

b) A – Finding Nemo
   Hinweis: Finding Nemo *ist für die ganze Familie.*

c) C – Titanic
   Hinweis: Titanic *ist ein Liebesfilm.*

d) B – The Matrix
   Hinweis: **The Matrix** *ist ein Actionfilm.*

e) A – Finding Nemo
   Hinweis: **Finding Nemo** *ist ein kindgerechter Film mit Tieren.*

f) C – Titanic
   Hinweis: **Titanic** *ist ein romantischer Film.*

g) D – Lord of the Rings
   Hinweis: **Lord of the Rings** *wurde in Neuseeland gedreht.*

h) A or C – Finding Nemo or Titanic
   Hinweis: *Diese beiden Filme laufen nachmittags.*

i) D – Lord of the Rings
   Hinweis: *J. R. R. Tolkien hat* **Lord of the Rings** *geschrieben.*

Aufgabe 2

Hinweis: *In dieser Aufgabe wird nach Details aus der Kinowerbung gefragt. Überlege gründlich, bevor du die Antworten ankreuzt.*

a) James Cameron

b) Hall 2

c) popcorn and a 0.3 l soft drink

d) The Matrix

e) Lord of the Rings I–III

f) Keanu Reeves

g) a clown fish

Aufgabe 3

Hinweis: *Es ist wichtig, dass du die Aufgabenstellungen immer sorgfältig durchliest. Sie enthalten alle wichtigen Informationen zum Lösen der Aufgabe.*

a) All these films have already been in the cinemas and are being shown again because of their great popularity.

b) After the film you can vote how you liked it. When you take part in the voting you can win tickets for free.

c) In the Pixar film studios.

d) Because there is only limited space for this event.

Reading Comprehension Test 3: Very trendy!

Aufgabe 1

a) false
   Hinweis: *siehe 1. Seite der Homepage*

b) false
   Hinweis: *siehe 1. Seite der Homepage*

c) false
   Hinweis: *siehe 1. und 2. Seite der Homepage*

d) true
   Hinweis: *siehe 3. Seite der Homepage*

e) not given

f) true
   Hinweis: *siehe alle Seiten der Homepage*

g) false
   Hinweis: *siehe 1. Seite der Homepage*

h) false
   Hinweis: *siehe 3. Seite der Homepage*

i) not given

j) false
   Hinweis: *siehe 3. Seite der Homepage*

k) true
   Hinweis: *siehe 1. Seite der Homepage*

Aufgabe 2

a) They sell clothes, shoes and accessories for boys and girls.
   Hinweis: *siehe 1. Seite der Homepage*

b) Because *trendshoes* are celebrating their 10th anniversary/jubilee.
   Hinweis: *siehe 1. Seite der Homepage*

c) The sneakers cost 29 £ (43,50 €).

d) With the newsletter you get the latest information about the new collection, all the fashion news and information about specials.
   Hinweis: *siehe 1. Seite der Homepage*

e) They have been popular for decades.
   Hinweis: *siehe 2. Seite der Homepage*

Aufgabe 3

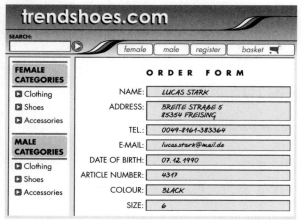

trendshoes.com

SEARCH:

| female | male | register | basket 🛒 |

FEMALE CATEGORIES
- ▶ Clothing
- ▶ Shoes
- ▶ Accessories

MALE CATEGORIES
- ▶ Clothing
- ▶ Shoes
- ▶ Accessories

O R D E R   F O R M

NAME:	*LUCAS STARK*
ADDRESS:	*BREITE STRAßE 5* *85354 FREISING*
TEL.:	*0049-8161-383364*
E-MAIL:	*lucas.stark@mail.de*
DATE OF BIRTH:	*07.12.1990*
ARTICLE NUMBER:	*4317*
COLOUR:	*BLACK*
SIZE:	*6*

Aufgabe 4

a) They offer free delivery <u>in</u> Europe.
   Hinweis: *siehe 1. Seite der Homepage*

b) The retro styled sneakers have been <u>popular</u> for decades.
   Hinweis: *siehe 2. Seite der Homepage*

c) They accept <u>payment</u> by credit card or per invoice.
   Hinweis: *siehe 3. Seite der Homepage*

d) They <u>provide</u> secure payment.
   Hinweis: *siehe 3. Seite der Homepage*

e) Defective <u>goods</u> are replaced without any costs for the customer.
   Hinweis: *siehe 3. Seite der Homepage*

Aufgabe 5

1	2	3	4	5	6	7
F	A	E	G	D	C	B

26

Aufgabe 1

a) false

Hinweis: *"After I had finished school,"* *(Z. 3 f.)*

b) false

Hinweis: *"I asked everyone to give me money"* *(Z. 8 f.)*;
"together with my savings from the job I took the summer before" *(Z. 10 f.)*

c) not given

d) false

Hinweis: *"book a flight to Sydney"* *(Z. 12 f.)*

e) not given

f) true

Hinweis: *"a special offer"* *(Z. 13 f.)*

g) true

Hinweis: *"beautiful, sunny day."* *(Z. 32 f.)*

h) true

Hinweis: *"I chose a youth hostel in Sydney which was especially for back-packers,"* *(Z. 35 ff.)*

i) not given

j) false

Hinweis: *"The backpackers were from all over the world"* *(Z. 44 f.)*

k) false

Hinweis: *"chose to do the rest of our journey together"* *(Z. 50 f.)*

l) true

Hinweis: *"the best idea I ever had"* *(Z. 56 f.)*; *"wouldn't have missed it for the world."* *(Z. 57 f.)*

m) true

Hinweis: *"spend one year of my apprenticeship down under"* *(Z. 63 ff.)*

Aufgabe 2

a) Her relatives gave her money as a present for passing her exams and she had savings from a job she took the summer before.

Hinweis: *Z. 8 ff.*

b) Her parents were not excited about Bettina's idea to travel alone through Australia. They gave in finally.
   Hinweis: *Z. 15ff. und Z. 21ff.*

c) Bettina went to Sydney, Perth, Melbourne and the outback.
   Hinweis: *Z. 25ff.*

d) She enjoyed her time in Australia because she met interesting people, stayed in an exciting country and had the opportunity to improve her English. She also learned to look after herself.
   Hinweis: *Z. 58 – 62*

Aufgabe 3

a) B
b) A
c) D
d) C

Allgemeiner Hinweis: *Für das gesamte Kapitel „Text Production" ist es wichtig, dass du dir die Arbeitsschritte zum Verfassen eines Aufsatzes auf Seite 43 genau durchliest und dementsprechend arbeitest. Wenn du nach diesen Schritten vorgehst, wird dir ein gut strukturierter Aufsatz bestimmt nicht mehr schwerfallen.*

Aufgabe 1

Hinweis: *Hier musst du noch keinen vollständigen Text schreiben, sondern die unterstrichenen Wörter durch Attribute näher beschreiben. Mit dieser Aufgabe sollst du für deine eigenen Aufsätze trainieren.*

a) The <u>beautiful</u> <u>house</u> at the end of the street belongs to my parents.

b) Grandma told me to throw the <u>old</u> <u>carpet</u> away.

c) James loves sitting in his room and listening to <u>loud</u> <u>music</u>.

d) Take off your <u>dirty</u> <u>shoes</u>!

e) I live in a <u>small</u> <u>village</u>.

f) I got a <u>dark</u> <u>blue</u> coat for my birthday.

g) We travelled a lot during our <u>summer</u> <u>holidays</u>.

Aufgabe 2

Hinweis: *Konjunktionen helfen dir, Sätze elegant zu verknüpfen und nicht nur aneinander zu reihen. Es ist bestimmt hilfreich, wenn du sie mit Beispielsätzen in deine Vokabelkartei aufnimmst. Zur deutschen Bedeutung der englischen Konjunktionen vergleiche die Kurzgrammatik auf S. 82 f.*

a) I took an umbrella with me this morning <u>because</u> it was raining.

b) <u>When</u>/<u>As soon as</u> I'm 18 years old I will leave home.

c) I'd love to visit New York, <u>but</u> I don't have enough money.

d) Jack moved to another town <u>in order to</u> become independent.

e) Clara washes the dishes <u>while</u> she's talking to her best friend on the phone.

Aufgabe 3

Hinweis: *Zu diesen Bildern musst du einen Dialog schreiben. Schaue dir also die Bilder genau an und verwende die deutschen Stichpunkte als Vorlage für deinen englischen Text. Denke daran, dass du hier gesprochene Sprache wiedergibst. Du kannst also verkürzte Formen und Umgangssprache verwenden.*

Bild 1

DAD: Ann, we're worried about your bad marks at school. That's why we want you to stop seeing your boyfriend Kevin.

MUM: Do you really want to repeat a year?

Bild 2

ANN: My parents are so strict. They don't want me to see you any more.

KEVIN: Don't worry, we'll work things out.

Bild 3

KEVIN: I'll wait for you till the exams are over.

ANN: Kevin, I love you.

Aufgabe 4

Hinweis: *Hier musst du noch keinen eigenen Text schreiben, sondern du kannst zunächst einmal üben, ein Bild zu beschreiben. Dazu musst du dir das Bild genau ansehen, um auch detaillierte Fragen beantworten zu können.*
Verwende die ing-Form, um zu beschreiben, was gerade geschieht.

a) It's on the coast of an island.

b) Behind the boat, there is a beach and a house. You can also see some people standing behind the boat.

c) A man with a child is standing in front of the boat.

d) He is standing in the water and looking down. He is probably holding the child's hand.

Aufgabe 5

a) The man is playing some musical instruments.

b) The man is standing in front of a shop in a town.

c) He is playing the guitar, a drum set and a harmonica.

d) There are some children standing behind the man. They are enjoying the music. One little girl is clapping her hands.

e) The man is wearing socks with the Union Jack on them. That is the British flag, so either he is from Great Britain or he just likes the socks.

Aufgabe 6

Hinweis: *Hier musst du nicht mehr nur beschreiben, sondern einen kleinen Text verfassen. Natürlich kannst du die Antworten aus Aufgabe 5 als Basis für den Text nehmen.*

A sample answer:
When I was walking along the high street yesterday, all of a sudden I saw a lot of people and heard some fantastic music. It was a man who was playing a drum set, a guitar and a harmonica all on his own. He looked very funny, because he was carrying the drum set on his back. All the people who were listening enjoyed his music very much.

Aufgabe 7

Hinweis: *Hier musst du eine Geschichte zu den Bildern schreiben. Zu den einzelnen Bildern hast du deutsche Stichworte, die dir helfen, eine kleine Geschichte zu schreiben. Deine Geschichte sollte nachvollziehbar sein, auch wenn man die Bilder nicht gesehen hat.*

A sample answer:
Mr Smith wants to eat some biscuits. He takes the box out of the cupboard but the box is empty. At once he goes to the cat with the empty box and screams at it furiously. Afterwards, he leaves the room, still very angry that he cannot eat biscuits that day. He goes into the kitchen to tell his wife about the biscuits. Mrs Smith is preparing some tea and biscuits. Suddenly, Mr Smith realizes that it wasn't the cat who ate the biscuits but that his wife had emptied the box to prepare the biscuits for tea. Mr Smith feels very guilty about how he treated the cat so he gives it a cake to apologise.

Aufgabe 8

Hinweis: *Die folgenden Lösungen sind lediglich Beispiele. Stelle dir vor, was du in einer realen Situation sagen würdest.*

a) No, I don't like maths. My favourite subject is geography.

b) Yes, please. I'd like five sausages, please.

c) My name is Paul. How are you?

d) No, I don't. I prefer going to the cinema.

e) Yes, I do. It's my favourite sport.

Aufgabe 9

Hinweis: *Versuche, möglichst englische Wendungen zu benutzen und nicht nur Wort für Wort zu übersetzen.*

TRAVEL AGENT: Hello, how can I help you?

YOU: *Hello. I would like some information on bike tours in Ireland. Do you have any brochures about tours like that?*

TRAVEL AGENT: When would you like to go?

YOU: *In the summer holidays.*

TRAVEL AGENT: Would you like to rent bikes there or are you going to take your own bikes?

YOU: *Could you give me some information for both possibilities? I'd like to compare prices at home and then decide.*

TRAVEL AGENT: No problem. Here you are. Don't hesitate to come back if you have any questions.

YOU: Thank you very much. Bye.

Aufgabe 10

Hinweis: *Die Wendungen auf Seite 44 ff. helfen dir, diese Aufgabe zu lösen. Es ist hilfreich, wenn du die Wendungen auswendig lernst.*

a) Dear (Aunt) Mary   Best wishes (Love)

b) Dear Mrs Smith   Yours sincerely

c) Dear Sir or Madam   Yours faithfully

d) Dear Luke   Best wishes (Love)

e) Dear Mr O'Brien   Yours sincerely

f) Dear Grandma and Granddad   Best wishes (Love)

g) Dear Sir or Madam   Yours faithfully

h) Dear Madam   Yours faithfully

Aufgabe 11

Hinweis: *Bei dieser Aufgabe sind einige Wörter und Wendungen vorgegeben, die dir bei der Orientierung und Strukturierung deiner Postkarte helfen. Auf Seite 44 f. findest du außerdem Wendungen für eine angemessene Begrüßung und einen angemessenen Schluss. Allgemein gilt, dass du z. B. beim Schreiben eines Briefes immer an den Empfänger denken musst: Ist es ein Freund oder guter Bekannter? Oder handelt es sich um einen geschäftlichen/offiziellen Brief? Was ist der Zweck dieses Briefes? Der Adressat des Briefes entscheidet darüber, welchen Ton, welche Wortwahl du benutzt. Lies dir die Aufgabenstellung immer genau durch. Sie enthält alle wichtigen Informationen, die du als Grundlage für einen guten Brief benötigst.*

7/7/08

Dear Anne,

How are you? Hello from the USA! We're having a lot of fun here. Yesterday I went to see the musical "The Lion King" with my family in Minskoff Theatre in New York. I liked the musical because of the great music, the fantastic dancers and singers and the interesting costumes. But the tickets were quite expensive. We're going to stay in New York for one more day, then we're flying to Florida.

I'll give you a call as soon as I'm home again.

Best wishes,

(your name)

Aufgabe 12

Hinweis: *Lies dir den Einleitungstext und die Anzeige genau durch. Die Angaben helfen dir, die Sätze sinnvoll zu ergänzen.*

(address)
(date)

Mr Tom Leary
Hotel Bellevue
63 London Road
St Albans
AL5 6 PH

Dear Mr Leary,

I am interested in working at <u>Hotel Bellevue over the summer</u>. My name is ... ,
I'm ... years old and I live in ... , Germany. I attend the 5th form *(entspricht der 9..
Klasse)*. After finishing school I would like to work <u>in a hotel</u>. The job at your
hotel would be a great opportunity to <u>gain some experience</u>.
Could you please give me some more information about the job?
How long <u>would I have to work every day</u>? How much <u>do you pay</u>?
I look forward <u>to hearing from you</u>.

Yours sincerely,

(signature)

(your name)

Aufgabe 13

Hi Julian,

How are you? Thanks a lot for your e-mail. I'm really happy because I got a job at
a hotel in Cambridge for the holidays. That's great, isn't it? I will have to clean the
rooms or support the staff at reception and I'll have to help out in the kitchen.
I'm glad that I will earn some money. Afterwards I will still have one week left of
my holidays and I would love to spend it in Dublin with you. I would like to
come the last week of August and I'm looking forward to the festival which you
told me about.

Best wishes,

(your name)

Aufgabe 14

Hinweis: *Für den tabellarischen Lebenslauf genügt es, wenn du in Stichpunkten
antwortest. Beim Punkt „Education" gibst du deine Klassenstufe (die 9. Klasse entspricht der „5th form") und Schulart an (die Hauptschule entspricht ungefähr einer
„Secondary School" in England; die Grundschule heißt „Primary School"). Gib
auch besondere Fähigkeiten an, die für den Job nützlich sein könnten (z. B. good at
organizing/maths/calculating/using the computer). Die Angabe deiner Hobbies
rundet deinen Lebenslauf ab (z. B. travelling, reading, playing football/soccer).*

Springdale Post
24 Western Street
Springdale
SP 1 5NW

ad number 452678

Dear Sir or Madam,

I would like to apply for the summer job in your dry cleaning shop. My name is ... and I am ... years old. I am a pupil from Germany and I will spend my summer holiday with a host family in Springdale. I would like to earn some money for my holiday. Your ad is interesting for me because I have already worked in a dry cleaning shop in Germany. I enjoyed the work there. I am reliable, always ready to help and good at organizing. Talking to the customers would also help me to practise my English.

Can you tell me how long the working hours in your shop are?

I would really enjoy working with you and hope to hear from you soon.

Yours faithfully,

(signature)
(your name)

✦ **Allgemeiner Hinweis:** *Du findest Aufgaben zu allen Bereichen der mündlichen*
✦ *Prüfung. Lies die Aufgabenstellungen genau durch, aber beachte, dass du sie in der*
✦ *Prüfung nicht vorgelegt bekommst. In der Prüfung werden die Aufgaben und Fra-*
✦ *gen ausschließlich mündlich an dich gerichtet.*

Aufgabe 1

✦ **Hinweis:** *Deine Aufgabe ist es, die Abbildungen zu beschreiben und anschließend*
✦ *die Fragen des Prüfers zu beantworten.*

SCHÜLER: The picture shows a man who is ironing[1] a shirt. There is a big pile[2] of
shirts and other clothes behind him. He has a lot of work and doesn't look
happy. In the room behind him there is a woman who is sitting and watching
television. The woman is smiling.

PRÜFER: What relationship[3] do you think that the man and the woman have?

SCHÜLER: They are probably[4] husband and wife.

PRÜFER: Why do you think the man is unhappy?

SCHÜLER: He is unhappy because he has to iron the clothes while his wife is
watching television. Maybe[5] he would also like to watch TV.

PRÜFER: And why do you think the woman is smiling?

SCHÜLER: The woman is smiling because she doesn't have to work and can watch
TV. Maybe[5] she is also happy because her husband is doing the work.

PRÜFER: What do you think about this scene?

SCHÜLER: It is funny because in families you normally expect that the wife irons
the clothes and the husband doesn't do the housework. You would expect the
husband to watch TV and his wife do all the housework.

PRÜFER: Why do you think that usually[6] only the women work at home and not
the men?

SCHÜLER: I think that men don't like to work at home because when they grew
up, their fathers didn't work at home either and their mothers did all the
housework. They copy their parents' behaviour.

1	(to) iron: bügeln	4	probably: wahrscheinlich
2	pile: Stapel	5	maybe: vielleicht
3	relationship: Beziehung	6	usually: für gewöhnlich

Aufgabe 2

Hinweis: *Beschreibe das Foto und beantworte die Fragen des Prüfers.*

SCHÜLER: There are two girls sitting on a wall. Behind the wall there is a street where cars are passing by[1]. On the wall is a sign that reads "do not sit or stand on wall". The girl on the left side looks like she is waiting for somebody. The girl on the right looks happy.

PRÜFER: Why do you think that there is the sign on the wall?

SCHÜLER: It is there because the wall is right next to the street and because the passing cars can be dangerous for pedestrians[2].

PRÜFER: Do you think that the two girls are friends?

Schüler: No.

PRÜFER: Why?

SCHÜLER: Because they are sitting far apart from each other and the girl on the left side is looking in the other direction[3].

PRÜFER: What do you think about this picture?

SCHÜLER: It is funny because the two girls are sitting on the wall although[4] they are not allowed to.

PRÜFER: Do you think that they didn't read the sign?

SCHÜLER: It could be that they didn't read the sign. But maybe they have read the sign and just don't care.

1 (to) pass by: vorbeifahren
2 pedestrian: Fußgänger
3 direction: Richtung
4 although: obwohl

Aufgabe 3

Hinweis: *Übertrage vom Englischen ins Deutsche und umgekehrt. Denke daran, dass du nicht wortwörtlich übersetzen musst. Manchmal musst du die Personalpronomen verändern, z. B. von „I" zu „he" oder „she".*

PHARMACIST (A WOMAN): Good morning, how can I help you?

DU ZU DEINER OMA: **Die Apothekerin fragt wie sie uns helfen kann.**

OMA ANNELIESE: Könntest du der Apothekerin sagen, dass mir die Füße wehtun?

DU ZUR APOTHEKERIN: **My grandmother's feet are hurting.**

PHARMACIST: Did your grandmother have these problems before?

DU ZU DEINER OMA: **Hattest du vorher schon mal dieses Problem?**

OMA ANNELIESE: Nein.

DU ZUR APOTHEKERIN: **No, she didn't.**

PHARMACIST: Is there any problem with her shoes?

DU ZU DEINER OMA: **Kann es an deinen Schuhen liegen?**

OMA ANNELIESE: Nein. Mit meinen Schuhen ist alles in Ordnung. Die trage ich immer.

DU ZUR APOTHEKERIN: **No, everything is o.k. with her shoes. She always wears them.**

OMA ANNELIESE: Kann sie mir etwas geben die Schmerzen geben?

DU ZUR APOTHEKERIN: **Could you give her something against the pain?**

PHARMACIST: Well, I think your grandmother should see a doctor.

DU ZU DEINER OMA: **Die Apothekerin meint, du musst zum Arzt gehen.**

PHARMACIST: There is a very good doctor next door. Why don't you go there?

DU ZU DEINER OMA: **Nebenan gibt es einen guten Arzt. Wollen wir nicht dort hingehen?**

OMA ANNELIESE: Vielen Dank. Das ist eine gute Idee!

DU ZUR APOTHEKERIN: **Thank you very much! That's a very good idea.**

PHARMACIST: Good luck and good bye!

DU ZU DEINER OMA: **Alles Gute und auf Wiedersehen.**

Aufgabe 4

✎ **Hinweis:** *Übertrage wieder vom Englischen ins Deutsche und umgekehrt. Denke an die Veränderung der Personalpronomen, wenn nötig.*

RECEPTIONIST: Good afternoon. What can I do for you?

Guten Tag. Der Rezeptionist fragt, was er für Sie tun / wie er Ihnen helfen kann.

GERMAN TOURIST: Schmidt, guten Tag. Ich habe eine Reservierung.

Good afternoon. This is Mr. Schmidt. / He's Mr. Schmidt.[1] He's made a reservation.

RECEPTIONIST: Mr. Schmidt. Your reservation is from the fifteenth to the eighteenth of August. Could I have your passport and your credit card, please?

Mr. Schmidt. Sie haben vom 15. bis zum 18. August reserviert. Der Rezeptionist braucht Ihren Pass und Ihre Kreditkarte.

GERMAN TOURIST: Hier, bitte. Können Sie uns morgen um 6:00 Uhr aufwecken?

Here you are. Could you please wake them up at 6 o'clock in the morning?

RECEPTIONIST: Sure! Here's your key. Your room is number 223. Breakfast is served from 6 to 10 a.m. The breakfast room is on the first floor[2].

Das macht er gerne! Hier ist Ihr Schlüssel. Ihr Zimmer hat die Nummer 223. Von 6 Uhr bis 10 Uhr gibt es Frühstück. Der Frühstücksraum befindet sich im Erdgeschoss.

GERMAN TOURIST: Können wir im Hotel auch Karten für das Musical „Lion King"
kaufen?

Can Mr. Schmidt buy tickets for the musical "Lion King" at the hotel?

RECEPTIONIST: Sorry. We don't sell theatre tickets. You can buy them at the theatres on Broadway or at the ticket office on Times Square.

**Es tut ihm leid, aber hier im Hotel werden keine Theaterkarten verkauft.
Sie können sie aber in den Theatern am Broadway oder am Ticketstand am
Times Square erwerben.**

GERMAN TOURIST: Danke. Auf Wiedersehen.

Thank you. Goodbye.

1   Übertrage deutsche Nachnamen **nicht** ins Englische
2   First floor: Erdgeschoss

Aufgabe 5

✎ **Hinweis:** *Dolmetsche zwischen der deutschen Touristin und der Verkäuferin.*

ASSISTANT: Hello, can I help you?

Die Verkäuferin fragt, ob sie Ihnen helfen kann.

GERMAN TOURIST: Ja, bitte. Ich hätte dieses T-Shirt gerne in Blau.

Yes, please. She would like to have this T-shirt in blue, please.

ASSISTANT: Here you are.

Hier, bitte schön.

GERMAN TOURIST: Wo kann ich es anprobieren?

Where can she try it on?

ASSISTANT: The changing rooms are over there.

Die Umkleidekabinen sind dort drüben.

GERMAN TOURIST: Dieses T-Shirt ist zu groß. Kann ich ein Kleineres haben?

This T-shirt is too large (for her). Could she have a smaller one, please?

(Nach dem Anprobieren)

Jetzt passt es.

This one fits!

ASSISTANT: Would you like anything else?

Brauchen Sie sonst noch etwas? / Kann sie sonst noch etwas für Sie tun?

GERMAN TOURIST: Ich nehme auch diese beiden Postkarten. Verkaufen Sie auch
Briefmarken?

**These postcards, please. / She wants to have these postcards, too. Do you
sell stamps?**

ASSISTANT: No, I'm sorry. You have to buy them at the post office.

Leider nein. Die können Sie nur im Postamt kaufen.

GERMAN TOURIST: Schade. Trotzdem danke und auf Wiedersehen.
What a pity. Anyway, thanks for your help. Goodbye.

Aufgabe 6

✎ **Hinweis:** *Verbinde wieder die Stichpunkte zu einem kleinen Vortrag. Achte darauf, dass du alle vorgegebenen Stichpunkte verwendest und dass dein Vortrag einen „roten Faden" hat.*

Telling about a trip

Last August my friend and his parents went on a holiday to England, where they went on a bike tour.

They stayed in England for two weeks. They rented[1] the bikes in Bristol. There they started the tour along the coast. They wanted to go camping as well, but they weren't able to because it was too cold. So they stayed in hotels instead. The weather was bad: They had only two sunny days and a lot of rain instead. In the end, my friend's bike was stolen at the train station.

My friend was happy when the holiday was over.

1 (to) rent: mieten

Aufgabe 7

✎ **Hinweis:** *Bilde anhand der Stichpunkte Fragen und Antworten für das Verkaufsgespräch. Achte auch hier wieder darauf, dass dein Gespräch logisch aufgebaut ist.*

PRÜFER: Hello boys, how can I help you?

SCHÜLER: Are there still tickets for "Harry Potter" available?

PRÜFER: Yes, there are. How many would you like to have?

SCHÜLER: Three, please.

PRÜFER: The tickets for the back rows are £ 6 each, the tickets for the front rows £ 4. Which tickets would you like to have?

SCHÜLER: We would like to have the front row tickets for £ 4, please.

PRÜFER: Here you are. That's £ 12. Is there anything else I can do for you?

SCHÜLER: Yes, please. At what time does the film start?

PRÜFER: The film starts at 7 o'clock. That's in 20 minutes.

SCHÜLER: Where can we buy some popcorn and a coke?

PRÜFER: You can buy them at the bar over there. If you want to buy a film poster, you can get it here at the ticket counter. Do you want one?

SCHÜLER: No thanks, bye.

Aufgabe 8

✐ **Hinweis:** *Verbinde die Stichpunkte zu einem kleinen Dialog. Achte darauf, dass du*
✐ *alle vorgegebenen Stichpunkte verwendest und dass dein Dialog sinnvoll ist.*

YOU: Hi, where are you from?

BOY: Hi there, nice to meet you, our group is from Manchester, England.

YOU: Are you here on a holiday?

BOY: No, we're not. We are here for a student exchange[1] with a German school.

YOU: Do you like the music?

BOY: Yeah, it's great!

YOU: You know what? I was about to go for a drink, do you want something?

BOY: Yes, I'd like a coke, please.

YOU: Sure, I'll get it.

BOY: By the way, what's your name? I'm Dylan.

YOU: I'm ... Just a moment, I'll be right back.

1 Schüleraustausch

Aufgabe 9

✐ **Hinweis:** *Denke daran, dein Referat klar zu gliedern:*
✐ **Einleitung:** *Gib an, worüber du dein Referat hältst und warum du dieses Thema*
✐ *gewählt hast. Zur Veranschaulichung kannst du z. B. ein Harry-Potter-Buch, ein*
✐ *Filmplakat oder ein Foto von J. K. Rowling mitbringen.*
✐ **Hauptteil:** *Unterteile dein Referat in Sinnabschnitte, z. B. Leben von J. K. Rowling*
✐ *vor dem Erfolg, der Erfolg der Harry-Potter-Bücher, Leben von J. K. Rowling mit*
✐ *dem Erfolg. Dein Referat sollte alle wichtigen Informationen zu J. K. Rowling ent-*
✐ *halten. Die Angaben müssen richtig sein. Informiere dich deshalb gründlich, z. B. im*
✐ *Internet.*
✐ **Schluss:** *Am Ende des Referats kannst du nochmals deine eigene Meinung nennen.*
✐ *Der Schluss kann auch ein Fazit/eine Zusammenfassung des Gesagten in einem*
✐ *Satz enthalten.*
✐ *In der Prüfung könnten folgende Fragen gestellt werden: Why do you think that so*
✐ *many people around the world are Harry Potter fans? What do you like about J. K.*
✐ *Rowling? You like reading. What other hobbies do you have? What does it mean*
✐ *when you have to "raise a child on your own"?*

Like many people, I am a great fan of Harry Potter. I have read all of the Harry Potter books and seen the films in the cinema. Today I would like to tell you a few things about the person who invented Harry Potter, the British author Joanne Kathleen Rowling.

Better known as J. K. Rowling, she was born in Yate, England, in 1965. She grew up in Chepstow in Wales and then went to study French at Exeter University. As a student, she also spent a year in Paris. Later, J. K. Rowling moved to London to work for the human rights organization[1] Amnesty International.

J. K. Rowling had the idea of Harry Potter while she was on a train from Manchester to London in 1990. As she did not earn any money as an author at that time, she could only write in her free time. J. K. Rowling studied to become a teacher and moved to Portugal, where she taught English. She got married and had a baby. But later she had to raise[2] the child by herself. Sometimes she was only able to write the Harry Potter book when her little daughter was sleeping.

Before publishing[3] the first book, J. K. Rowling had very little money. While she was still studying to become a teacher, she and her baby had to live on 70 pounds a week.

"Harry Potter and the Philosopher's Stone" was finally published in 1997 and was a great success[4]. Before that, lots of children had only been interested in television or computer games, but then they started to read again. But it was not just children who liked Harry Potter – their parents did, too. J. K. Rowling became one of the best-selling authors in the world. The seventh and final book, "Harry Potter and the Deathly Hallows", was sold 11 million times in the first day after the sales[5] started. It is the "fastest selling book in history". You can buy Harry Potter books in 200 countries and in 61 languages. The Harry Potter films have also been very successful.

J. K. Rowling has also won many international prizes for her books and become very rich. Today she has over 500 million pounds. I hope that she will continue to write books like those of Harry Potter!

1 human rights organization: Menschenrechtsorganisation
2 (to) raise: aufziehen
3 (to) publish: veröffentlichen
4 success: Erfolg
5 sale: Verkauf

Aufgabe 10

Hinweis: *Denke daran, dein Referat klar zu gliedern:*

Einleitung: *Nenne das Thema deines Referates und begründe, warum du es gewählt hast.*

Hauptteil: *Wenn du über einen Urlaub berichtest, kannst du wie hier der Reihe nach erzählen, was passiert ist, oder du suchst dir nur bestimmte wichtige Ereignisse aus, von denen du berichtest. Wenn du Fachbegriffe verwendest oder die Namen bestimmter Attraktionen nennst, solltest du erklären, was sie bedeuten bzw. was es dort zu sehen gibt. Bringe zur Veranschaulichung Fotos oder Souvenirs mit oder erstelle ein Plakat zum Referat.*

Schluss: *Fasse den Inhalt deines Referats kurz zusammen oder finde einen Schluss, der das Referat abrundet.*

In der Prüfung könnten folgende Fragen gestellt werden: What activity did you like best and why? How old is your sister and what did she enjoy? What souvenirs did you and your sister get at the flea market? Why did you like the Epcot Center?

I would like to tell you about the fantastic holiday I spent with my family this summer. My parents, my sister and I spent three weeks in Florida, which is a very exciting place to see.

In the middle of August, we flew to Miami. Because we had to change planes in Chicago, the trip took 15 hours and we were very tired when we arrived. My parents rented[1] a car at the airport and we drove to a holiday flat[2] in Fort Lauderdale, where we all fell into bed. The next day, we all wanted to go to the beach first, so we drove to Miami Beach where we had a beach picnic for lunch. But it was too hot! It was 36 to 38 degrees and you had to wear sandals when walking in the sand, because it was so hot! But my sister and I ran into the sea and it was great!

For the first week we stayed in Fort Lauderdale. We went to the beach and sometimes we went on a trip. In Miami we saw the Seaquarium, where they do shows with killer whales and dolphins. We also went to a parrot park, where we saw thousands of colourful birds. Some birds even sat down on the visitors and we took a lot of photos there. Once, we also went to a big flea market in Fort Lauderdale, where we stayed for the whole afternoon. My sister and I bought some souvenirs there.

In the second week, we first drove to Orlando, which is in the middle of Florida, where we stayed in a motel for a couple of days. We went to different fun parks like Disney World and the MGM Studios. But I liked the Epcot Center best. It is a big park where you can go on different rides but also see a lot of interesting films or shows about other cultures, nature or animals. The next time I go to Florida, I will go to the Epcot Center again for sure! After Orlando, we drove to the

Lyndon B. Johnson Space Center, where we lost my sister and had to look for her for 2 hours before we found her again. So we didn't see all of the spaceships. We then spent a few more days at the beach.

At the end of our holiday, my father wanted to drive to Key West. We drove for a whole day, and at the end of the trip we crossed a lot of bridges which go right over the ocean. In Key West we went to the spot which is the southernmost tip[3] of the USA. We bought more souvenirs and went to see a museum about treasure hunting[4] in the sea. We also saw the house of Ernest Hemingway, the famous author.

We were all sad when we had to drive back to the airport in Miami. But my parents promised that we would travel to Florida again soon!

1   (to) rent: mieten
2   flat: Apartment
3   southernmost tip: das südlichste Ende
4   treasure hunting: Schatzsuchen

Aufgabe 11

a) Keira Knightley has acted in Star Wars Episode I, Bend It Like Beckham and Pirates of the Caribbean.

b) *(Your personal answer)* I saw all the *Pirates of the Caribbean* films. I think they are great! I hope they will produce another part, soon!

c) Yes, Keira earns money as a model (on television and working for Chanel).

d) *(Your personal answer)* I think she is a good actress and a beautiful woman. She's still young but already very successful.

Aufgabe 12

1. Men started to wear skirts again in the second half of the 20th century.

2. There are only a few expensive brands, so it is not possible to buy men's skirts in every clothing store. *(Or your personal answer from your own shopping experience.)*

3. *(Your personal answer)* I have never seen a man in my town wearing a men's skirt, but I once saw a photo in a magazine of a famous star wearing a skirt. I think it was David Beckham.

4. *(Your personal answer)* In my opinion men should wear trousers when they go to work. But in their free time they could wear a skirt. I'm sure that a man who wears a skirt at the disco or in a pub would get a lot of attention!

Listening

Allgemeiner Hinweis: *Zur Bearbeitung des Hörtextes verwendest du die beiliegende CD oder du lässt dir die Texte vorlesen. Du hörst vier kurze Dialoge. Jede der zugehörigen Aufgaben bezieht sich auf einen der Dialoge, sodass du die richtigen Lösungen der Reihe nach ankreuzen kannst. Höre die Hörtexte genau an und mache Notizen, wenn du möchtest. Schaue in die Textvorlage, wenn du gar nicht mehr weiterkommst.*

Tapescript 1: Susie is phoning her boyfriend Robert

SUSIE: Hi, Robert! It's me, Susie. What are we doing on Simon's birthday? It's this Thursday, remember?

ROBERT: Oh gosh! I totally forgot about that! What could we do? Have you got any ideas?

SUSIE: Why don't we invite him and Helen to dinner at a nice restaurant?

ROBERT: Okay. How about that new Mexican restaurant?

SUSIE: Good idea. Can you book[1] a table for us?

ROBERT: Sure. I'll book a table for 7.30. Is that all right?

SUSIE: Fine. Can you pick me up after work?

ROBERT: No problem. See you on Thursday.

1 (to) book – buchen

a) Thursday.
   Hinweis: Z. 2

b) a Mexican restaurant.
   Hinweis: Z. 6

c) 7.30.
   Hinweis: Z. 8

Tapescript 2: Helen is phoning a ticket hotline

HOTLINE: Sydney Ticket Service. Can I help you?

HELEN: Yes, I'd like two tickets for the Kylie Minogue concert next Saturday, please.

HOTLINE: Okay. Would you like seats or standing room tickets?

HELEN: How much are they?

5 HOTLINE: The seats are 25 dollars and standing room tickets are 30 dollars.

HELEN: Why are standing room[1] tickets more expensive?

HOTLINE: Well, you're closer to the stage and you can see Kylie much better.

HELEN: Oh, I see. Then I'd like two standing room tickets, please. Can I pay by credit card?

10 HOTLINE: Yes, you can pay cash or by credit card when you pick up the tickets.

HELEN: Okay, thank you very much, goodbye.

1 standing room ticket – Stehplatzkarte

a) false
  Hinweis: Z. 2

b) true
  Hinweis: Z. 6

c) true
  Hinweis: Z. 9

Tapescript 3: Robert meets Simon at the concert

1 ROBERT: Hi, Simon. What a surprise to meet you here at a Kylie Minogue concert. Are you enjoying it?

SIMON: Yes, it's much better than I thought. She's a great singer.

ROBERT: Yeah, I think so, too.

5 SIMON: Helen has been a fan for many years. Now she wants to buy a Kylie Minogue T-shirt. Do you know if there's a souvenir stand here?

ROBERT: Yes, there's one round the corner. I've just bought a poster there.

SIMON: Oh, thanks, Robert. I'm sure I can get a T-shirt there, too.

ROBERT: Well, enjoy the rest of the concert. Bye.

a) Robert
  Hinweis: Z. 2

b) Simon
  Hinweis: Z. 5

c) Robert
  Hinweis: Z. 7

HELEN: Hi, darling, how was work today?

SIMON: I'm so tired. I really need a holiday!

HELEN: Me, too. Guess what! When I was in town today I went to a travel agency[1] and picked up some catalogues. Look!

SIMON: Great! So you'd like to go to Hawaii?

HELEN: Yes, I've always wanted to see Waikiki Beach.

SIMON: Yes, I know. And I'm sure you want to try surfing. But I don't want to spend all my time at the beach. I'd like to visit some of the other Hawaiian islands, too.

HELEN: Okay. Let's look at the catalogues and see what they offer[2].

1 travel agency – Reisebüro
2 (to) offer – anbieten

a) to a travel agency
   Hinweis: Z. 3

b) Waikiki Beach
   Hinweis: Z. 6

c) visit other Hawaiian islands
   Hinweis: Z. 8/9

Use of English

Aufgabe 1

Hinweis: Hier wird dein Wortschatz überprüft. Du kannst zunächst überlegen, wie der gesuchte Begriff auf Deutsch heißt. Dann fällt dir der entsprechende englische Begriff bestimmt leichter ein.

a) library

b) dictionary

c) ferry

d) passport

e) map

Aufgabe 2

Hinweis: Beim Üben zu Hause kannst du die Wörter laut aufsagen. In der Prüfung kannst du die Worte leise vor dich hin flüstern, damit dir das Unterscheiden der Laute leichter fällt.

a) luck

Hinweis: Die übrigen Wörter werden mit [uː] ausgesprochen.

b) small

Hinweis: Die übrigen Wörter werden mit [æ] ausgesprochen.

c) swim

Hinweis: Die übrigen Wörter werden mit [aɪ] ausgesprochen.

d) bear

Hinweis: Die übrigen Wörter werden mit [ɪə] ausgesprochen.

Aufgabe 3

Hinweis: Lies dir nach dem Einsetzen immer den kompletten Satz noch einmal durch und überlege, ob er so sinnvoll und logisch ist.

a) because

b) While

Hinweis: *Für das deutsche Wort „während" gibt es im Englischen folgende Wör-ter: „while" → es ereignet sich etwas, während eine andere Handlung bereits im Verlauf ist ("While she was waiting, her mobile phone rang.");*
„during" → verwendest du, um einen Zeitrahmen anzugeben ("During our stay in Canada, we met some interesting people.")

c) Although

d) but (auch: although)

Aufgabe 4

Hinweis: *Zur Wortstellung in Aussagesätzen und Fragen schaue dir noch einmal die Seite 90 in der Kurzgrammatik an.*

a) Have you ever been to Australia?
   Hinweis: *Warst du schon einmal in Australien?*
   Beginne mit dem Hilfsverb „have", da du einen Fragesatz bildest.

b) You can go swimming in the sea in summer.
   In summer you can go swimming in the sea.
   Hinweis: *Im Sommer kann man im Meer schwimmen.*
   Die Zeitangabe „in summer" kann am Satzanfang oder am Satzende stehen.

c) I don't like to go shopping in my free time.
   In my free time I don't like to go shopping.
   Hinweis: *In meiner Freizeit gehe ich nicht gerne zum Einkaufen.*
   Die Zeitangabe „in my free time" kann am Satzanfang oder am Satzende stehen.

d) Two years ago we met Joe in Canada.
   We met Joe in Canada two years ago.
   Hinweis: *Vor zwei Jahren trafen wir Joe in Kanada.*
   Die Zeitangabe „two years ago" kann am Satzanfang oder am Satzende stehen.

Aufgabe 5

Hinweis: *Für jedes falsch geschriebene Wort wird ein halber Punkt abgezogen.*

a) yourself

b) herself

c) ourselves

d) themselves
   Hinweis: *the people = they → themselves*

Aufgabe 6

d	f	e	b	a	c

a) Did you enjoy the meal?
   Hinweis: *Hat Ihnen das Essen geschmeckt?*

b) A glass of mineral water, please.
   Hinweis: *Bitte ein Glas Mineralwasser.*

c) Yes, it was delicious. Can I have the bill, please?
   Hinweis: *Danke, es war köstlich! Kann ich bitte die Rechnung haben?*

d) Are you ready to order, madam?
   Hinweis: *Wollen Sie bestellen?*

e) And would you like a drink?
   Hinweis: *Möchten Sie etwas zu trinken?*

f) Yes, I'd like the chicken, please.
   Hinweis: *Ja, ich hätte gerne das Hähnchen.*

Aufgabe 7

Hinweis: *Vorsicht: verwechsle nicht „desserts" (Nachtische) mit „deserts" (Wüsten).*

0	Last year	1	as a cook	2	the desserts.
1	I worked	3	my job	0	a good summer job.
2	In the mornings	0	I had	3	very much.
3	I enjoyed	2	I prepared	1	from 9 am till 1 pm.

Aufgabe 8

Hinweis: *Wenn du beim Abschreiben Fehler machst, die den Sinn stark verändern, werden dir Punkte abgezogen.*

A: Would you <u>like to go</u> to the cinema on Friday evening?

Hinweis: *Möchtest du am Freitag ins Kino gehen?*

B: I'm sorry, but I'll <u>have to stay</u> at home and <u>look after</u> my little sister.

Hinweis: *Es tut mir leid, aber ich muss zu Hause bleiben und auf meine kleine Schwester aufpassen.*

A: <u>What about</u> your parents?

Hinweis: *Was ist mit deinen Eltern?*

B: They <u>are having dinner</u> at a restaurant that evening.

Hinweis: *Sie gehen an diesem Abend in ein Restaurant zum Abendessen.*

A: Oh, what a pity! Peter says there is an <u>exciting</u> movie at the Roxy.

Hinweis: *Wie schade! Pete sagte, dass ein aufregender Film im Roxy läuft.*

B: But why <u>don't you</u> come to my house instead? We <u>could watch</u> some videos.

Hinweis: *Warum kommst du nicht einfach zu mir nach Hause? Wir könnten zusammen Videos anschauen.*

A: Great idea! I'll bring some crisps and <u>some bottles of</u> lemonade.

Hinweis: *Das ist eine großartige Idee. Ich bringe Chips und Limonade mit.*

Reading

Allgemeiner Hinweis: *Die Arbeitszeit für die Teile C und D beträgt insgesamt 60 Minuten. Ein Wörterbuch darf verwendet werden.*

Vokabelhinweise:

nickname (Z. 4): Spitzname

loads (Z. 6): Lasten

climate (Z. 9): Klima

transcontinental (Z. 17/18): über den Kontinent

tracks (Z. 23): Gleise

run to (Z. 24): (hier) *verlaufen bis*

landscape (Z. 47): Landschaften

sleeper cabin (Z. 59): Schlafwagen

air conditioning (Z. 60): Klimaanlage(-n)

buffet car (Z. 63): Speisewagen

freight train (Z. 70): Güterzug

goods (Z. 74): Güter

road train (Z. 75): (nur in Australien): *Lastwägen mit mehreren Anhängern*

completion (Z. 77): Fertigstellung

Aufgabe 1

a) almost 3000 kilometres long.
   Hinweis: Z. 13

b) in the north.
   Hinweis: Z. 17

c) Adelaide.
   Hinweis: Z. 28

d) two or three times a week.
   Hinweis: Z. 42/43

e) air conditioning.
   Hinweis: Z. 60

f) a drink.
   Hinweis: Z. 65

Aufgabe 2

Hinweis: *Rechtschreibfehler führen bei dieser Aufgabe nicht zu Punktabzug.*

a) Because they were able to work in the hot Australian climate.
   Hinweis: *Z. 8/9*

b) Two days
   Hinweis: *Z. 13*

c) It had many bends and there were often problems with floods and heavy rain which washed away bridges and parts of the track.
   Hinweis: *Z. 20 ff.*

d) Green fields, red deserts, tropical forests
   Hinweis: *Z. 47 ff.*

e) In the restaurant, in the buffet car
   Hinweis: *Z. 62 ff.*

Aufgabe 3

0	1	2	3	4	5
B	D	A	C	F	E

Aufgabe 4

Hinweis: *Abschreibfehler führen bei dieser Aufgabe nicht zu Punktabzug.*

a) "The Ghan" is a legend in Australian history.
   Hinweis: *Z. 1/2*

b) Later they also transported materials for the new railway line.
   Hinweis: *Z. 9 ff.*

c) Many travellers leave the train in Alice Springs to visit the famous Ayers Rock.
   Hinweis: *Z. 52 ff.*

d) Freight trains as long as 1.8 kilometres carry hundreds of containers with products.
   Hinweis: *Z. 70 ff.*

Text Production

1. Correspondence: E-Mail

Hinweis: Die offenere Aufgabenstellung und die in Stichpunkten formulierten Angaben ermöglichen dir eine größere Freiheit in der Gestaltung der E-Mail. Die angegebene Lösung ist ein Beispiel.

Dear Mr and Mrs Spencer, Lucy and Tim,

Thank you very much for the email and the nice photos you sent. I will be arriving at Sydney airport on Monday, August 2nd, at 7:00 am[1]. Mrs Spencer, could you please tell me how to get from the airport to your house?

After the language course[2], I would like to travel in Australia. I would like to go to Ayers Rock and the Great Barrier Reef. Could you send me some information about the most interesting places to see[3]? I am also interested in doing[4] some sports and I hope to get to know some young Australians. What is there to do in the evenings? I am very excited about surfing but I am afraid of sharks. Are there many sharks in the ocean around Sydney? What is the weather like in August and September? Is it possible to go surfing at that time?

I am very happy to have the opportunity of travelling to Australia and I'm looking forward to meeting[5] you! Please write again soon!

Yours truly,

Alexandra

1 Beachte die Präpositionen on, at
2 language course – Sprachkurs
3 places to see; sights – Sehenswürdigkeiten
4 interested in do**ing** – Denke an die „ing"-Form.
5 looking forward to meet**ing** – Denke auch hier an die „ing"-Form.

2. Picture-based Writing (Bildfolge)

Hinweis: *Betrachte zunächst genau die Abbildungen. Außerdem findest du zu je-*
dem Bild der Bildergeschichte weitere Angaben. Verwende alle diese Informationen
für deinen Erzähltext.

A day in Sydney

Last August the Schmitt family from Germany spent their holiday in Australia.
On their first day in Sydney Mr and Mrs Schmitt, Max and Tina left the hotel at
9 am. They wanted to spend the day out[1], of course. At 10 am they arrived at the
Taronga Zoo, where they bought tickets for 30 A$ each. From 10 am to 1 pm
they explored[2] the Taronga Zoo and saw many animals, like kangaroos, emus and
crocodiles. Tina was happy, because she was allowed to pet[3] a koala bear. At
lunchtime they ate hot dogs and cake in a restaurant. Later, in the afternoon, they
went to the beach. Although it was very windy there, Mr Schmitt took a photo of
Max with a surfboard. Tina played soccer with her mother. Finally, in the evening, the Schmitt family was back in their hotel room. While Mr Schmitt and the
children watched television, Mrs Schmitt wrote postcards to the family back at
home in Germany.

1 (to) spend the day out – den Tag im Freien verbringen
2 (to) explore – erkundigen, ansehen
3 (to) pet – streicheln

Notenschlüssel

Notenstufen	1	2	3	4	5	6
Punkte	72 – 64	63,5 – 52	51,5 – 38	37,5 – 23	22,5 –12	11,5 – 0

Listening

Allgemeiner Hinweis: *Zur Bearbeitung des Hörtextes kannst du die beiliegende CD verwenden oder du lässt dir die Texte vorlesen. Du hörst vier kurze Dialoge. Jede der zugehörigen Aufgaben bezieht sich auf einen der Dialoge, sodass du die richtigen Lösungen der Reihe nach ankreuzen oder einsetzen kannst. Höre die Hörtexte genau an und mache Notizen, wenn du möchtest. Schaue nur ins Tapescript, wenn du gar nicht mehr weiterkommst.*

Tapescript 1: Mr Smith is phoning the Edinburgh Bed and Breakfast.

LANDLADY: Edinburgh Bed and Breakfast. Good afternoon, can I help you?

MR SMITH: Good afternoon. Would it be possible to make a reservation for next weekend?

LANDLADY: Let me check. Yes. What sort of room would you like?

5 MR SMITH: Well, there are three of us: my wife and I, and our nine-year-old daughter.

LANDLADY: I could offer you a double room with an extra bed for £ 75 per night, or a family room for £ 98 a night, including a full Scottish breakfast.

MR SMITH: Wonderful, I'll take the family room, please.

10 LANDLADY: Very well. May I have your name and credit card details, please?

a) next weekend
   Hinweis: *Z. 2 f.*

b) his wife and daughter.
   Hinweis: *Z. 5 f.*

c) £ 98 a night
   Hinweis: *Z. 8 f.*

Tapescript 2: Mrs Smith is at a tourist office in Edinburgh.

MRS SMITH: Good morning. We're only here in Edinburgh for the weekend and we'd like to see as much of the city as possible. What would you recommend?

CLERK: Well, you might be interested in a guided walk through the historic city centre. It starts in twenty minutes if you'd like to join us.

5 MRS SMITH: That sounds like a good idea. What will we see on the tour?

CLARK: The tour begins with a visit to Edinburgh Castle. It's the main visitor attraction here, you know. From there, we'll see the sights in the Old Town. We'll walk along Edinburgh's oldest road. It's called "The Royal Mile" and it connects Edinburgh Castle with the Palace of Holyrood House.

10 MRS SMITH: What's Holyrood House?

CLERK: It's the royal palace where the Queen stays when she's in Edinburgh. But she's not here today, so we'll be able to have a guided tour of the palace. That'll be the end of our tour and you'll have seen as much as possible in your short visit to Edinburgh.

15 MRS SMITH: Good, we'll take three tickets.

1 e (Edinburgh Castle)
/ **Hinweis:** *Z. 6 f.*

2 d (Royal Mile)
/ **Hinweis:** *Z. 8 f.*

3 b (Palace of Holyrood House)
/ **Hinweis:** *Z. 12 f.*

Tapescript 3: The Smith family is staying at the Edinburgh Bed and Breakfast.

1 LANDLADY: Good morning. Did you sleep well?

MR SMITH: Like a baby! It's so nice and quiet here.

LANDLADY: What would you like for your breakfast, sir? Sausages and eggs with toast?

5 MR SMITH: Yes, sausages, eggs and some toast for me, please. My wife might just have some toast. She'll be down in a minute.

LANDLADY: And what about your daughter? Would she like some porridge?

MR SMITH: Yes, I think so. With milk, please.

LANDLADY: And to drink? Tea or coffee?

10 MR SMITH: Tea for my wife and coffee for me, please. And some orange juice for our daughter.

LANDLADY: Oh, I can see they're coming now. I'll be with you in a moment.

a) false
/ **Hinweis:** *Z. 2*

b) false
/ **Hinweis:** *Z. 5 f.*

c) true
/ **Hinweis:** *Z. 10*

Tapescript 4: The Smith family wants to check in for their flight home from Edinburgh.

1 MR SMITH: Hello, we'd like to check in for the flight to London, please.

FLIGHT ATTENDANT: Which one would that be, sir? The one leaving at 11.05 or 12.20?

MR SMITH: The one at 11.05.

5 FLIGHT ATTENDANT: Ok, that's flight number 3250. May I see your tickets, please?

MR SMITH: Here you are. Do you have three seats together?

FLIGHT ATTENDANT: Let me see ... Yes, I do. It's your lucky day.

MR SMITH: Oh, great. Can I carry this bag on board with me?

FLIGHT ATTENDANT: No, I'm really sorry, sir. It's simply too large. You'll have to

10 check it in, I'm afraid.

MR SMITH: Ok. We have two more bags to check in as well. Here they are.

FLIGHT ATTENDANT: Thanks. Here are your boarding passes. Boarding begins at 10.25. The flight departs at 11.05. First you'll need to pass through security. The security check is down the hall to your right. Have a good flight.

15 MR SMITH: Thank you.

a) 3250
Hinweis: Z. 5

b) 3
Hinweis: Z. 9 ff.

c) 11.05
Hinweis: Z. 4 und 13

Use of English

Aufgabe 1

Hinweis: *Hier sind Wörter angegeben, die sich auf den ersten Blick sehr ähnlich sehen. Sage dir deshalb die Sätze mit dem jeweiligen Wort vor, dann erkennst du schneller, mit welchem Wort der Satz einen Sinn ergibt. Beachte hier u. a. grammatikalische Regeln wie die Bildung der Verbformen in den verschiedenen Zeiten.*

a) I don't feel <u>safe</u>.

b) He <u>fell</u> from the tree.

c) After the meal we had a delicious <u>dessert</u>.

d) I'm afraid he will <u>lose</u> his money.

Aufgabe 2

Ganesh is a genius. He is a <u>thirteen-year-old</u> boy and also the <u>youngest</u> person in Great Britain to have a university degree. All the university students are <u>older</u> than he is. Ganesh enjoys playing football with other teenagers of <u>his own age</u>.

Aufgabe 3

✔ **Hinweis:** *Hier sollst du das entsprechende Gegenteil (opposite) finden. Bei einer*
✔ *Aufgabe wie dieser hast du zudem einen Vorteil, wenn du dir einen großen Wort-*
✔ *schatz angeeignet hast, da du dann evtl. unter mehreren passenden Lösungen wäh-*
✔ *len kannst. Gib in der Prüfung nur eine Lösung an! Ist das richtige Wort jedoch*
✔ *falsch geschrieben, wird dir ein halber Punkt abgezogen.*

a) Most TV shows are <u>boring</u>, but watching a film in the cinema is <u>interesting/exciting</u>.

b) I always thought you were <u>clever/smart/intelligent</u>. But that was a <u>stupid</u> thing to say!

c) The train <u>leaves</u> Edinburgh at 10.30 a.m. – And when does it <u>arrive</u> in London?

d) Early in the morning Tom ran to the bus stop, but he didn't <u>catch/get</u> the bus. He <u>missed</u> it.

Aufgabe 4

0	Can you tell me what time the English lesson starts?	4	Here you are.
1	Can you tell me the way to the station?	3	No, you can't. I've got to visit grandma.
2	Can I help you?	1	I'm sorry, I don't know the town.
3	Can I borrow your car tonight, mum?	0	Yes, at nine-thirty.
4	Can you pass me the water, please?		You're welcome.
		2	No thanks, I'm just looking.

Aufgabe 5

Hinweis: *Hier musst du die Regeln bei der Bildung von if-Sätzen beachten. Du kannst sie noch einmal in der Kurzgrammatik auf S. 78 f. nachlesen.*

a) If the weather is fine, Tom <u>will play</u> soccer.

b) If I <u>learn</u> the vocabulary for the English test, I will get a good mark.

c) Susan will go to England, if she <u>has</u> enough money.

Aufgabe 6

Hinweis: *Hier musst du die Verben u. a. in die richtige Zeit setzen. Achte dabei auf Signalwörter wie* yesterday, never before, usually *und* next week.

Susan's brother Tom, who <u>is</u> two years younger then she is, loves Harry Potter. Yesterday he <u>bought</u> the last Potter book and in the evening he read over 200 pages. He <u>said/says</u>, "I think *Harry Potter and the Deathly Hallows* is the best of the seven Potter books. I <u>have never read</u> such a good book before!" But Susan usually <u>doesn't like</u> reading fantasy stories. She prefers crime stories. Next week she <u>will go / is going to</u> the bookshop to buy a new thriller.

Aufgabe 7

Hinweis: *Wenn du beim Abschreiben Fehler machst, die den Sinn stark verändern, werden dir Punkte abgezogen.*

A: <u>Where</u> do you come from?

Hinweis: *Woher kommst du?*

B: I'm from Scotland. That's <u>in</u> Great Britain.

Hinweis: *Ich bin aus Schottland. Das ist in Großbritannien.*

A: Are you <u>travelling</u> alone or with your family?

Hinweis: *Reist du alleine oder mit deiner Familie?*

B: With my family. We're visiting my father's sister. She <u>lives</u> in Munich.

Hinweis: *Mit meiner Familie. Wir besuchen die Schwester meines Vaters. Sie wohnt in München.*

A: <u>Have you ever</u> been to Munich before?

Hinweis: *Warst du schon mal in München?*

B: Yes, we visited Munich two years <u>ago</u>.

Hinweis: *Ja, wir haben vor zwei Jahren München besucht.*

A: <u>Would</u> you like to come back to Germany again some time?

/ Hinweis: *Möchtest du gerne mal wieder nach Deutschland kommen?*

B: Sure. I've <u>never been</u> to the Oktoberfest! I really want to see that some day.

/ Hinweis: *Klar. Ich war noch nie auf dem Oktoberfest. Ich möchte es unbedingt mal*
/ *sehen.*

Reading

/ **Allgemeiner Hinweis:** *Die Arbeitszeit für die Teile C und D beträgt insgesamt*
/ *60 Minuten. Ein Wörterbuch darf verwendet werden.*

/ **Vokabelhinweise:**
/ *sorcerer (am. Engl.) (Z. 17): Zauberer*
/ *suspense (Z. 27): Spannung*
/ *enthusiasm (Z. 47): Begeisterung*
/ *to promote sth. (Z. 53 f.): etw. fördern*
/ *social welfare (Z. 78): Sozialhilfe*

Aufgabe 1

a) true
/   Hinweis: *Z. 15 ff.*

b) true
/   Hinweis: *Z. 26 ff.*

c) true
/   Hinweis: *Z. 60 f.*

d) false
/   Hinweis: *Z. 63 ff.*

e) not in the text

f) false
/   Hinweis: *Z. 84 f.*

Aufgabe 2

1	2	3	4	5	6	7
C	G	E	H	B	A	F

Aufgabe 3

Hinweis: *Wenn du Rechtschreibfehler machst, die den Sinn stark verändern, wird dir jeweils ein halber Punkt abgezogen.*

a) They didn't sleep because they spent the whole weekend reading (Harry Potter).
   Hinweis: *Z. 6 f.*
b) Many bookstores around the world would open at midnight.
   Often fans wore costumes and had parties at the bookstores.
   The books were even specially delivered by mail to people's homes at midnight.
   Hinweis: *Z. 31 ff.*
c) Some critics think that the books promote witchcraft.
   The books may be a bad influence on young people.
   Hinweis: *Z. 53 ff.*
d) Today J K Rowling is probably the richest woman in Britain.
   J K Rowling was unemployed and had to live on social welfare.
   Now she owns a big house and she can afford to go on holiday.
   Hinweis: *Z. 73 ff.*

Aufgabe 4

Hinweis: *Wenn du beim Abschreiben Fehler machst, die den Sinn stark verändern, wird dir jeweils ein halber Punkt abgezogen.*

a) A school boy who discovers that he is a wizard.
   Hinweis: *Z. 19 f.*
b) Children as well as adults enjoy reading them. / Both children and adults were fascinated by J K Rowling' story.
   Hinweis: *Z. 17 ff. und 42 ff.*
c) More than 350 million Harry Potter books have been sold.
   Hinweis: *Z. 50 f.*
d) She was unemployed. / She had to live on social welfare.
   Hinweis: *Z. 76 ff.*

Text Production

Allgemeiner **Hinweis:** *Wähle zwischen der E-Mail und der Bildergeschichte. Setze das zweisprachige Wörterbuch gezielt ein.*

1. Correspondence: E-Mail

Hinweis: *Hier sollst du unter Beweis stellen, dass du frei formulieren kannst. Achte jedoch darauf, alle angegeben Punkte zum Inhalt in deine Mail einzubauen. Die angegebene Lösung ist ein Beispiel.*

Dear Sir or Madam,

My name is ... I am ... years old and I live with my parents and my little sister in ... My family and I really love the Harry Potter books. We have read all of them and seen the films as well. That is why we would love to see the Harry Potter locations in England and Scotland this summer.

When we wanted to do the trip last year your tour was sold out. We were so disappointed. Now, I would like to ask you for some information about tours this year. Is it still possible to book a tour? How many days do the tours take?

We would really like to see the Harry Potter film locations in Scotland and Oxford. Are London or Edinburgh also included in the trip? Is there special accomodation that you offer for families? We would like to have accommodation that includes meals and has rooms with a shower or a bath.

Could you also send us some price lists, city maps and brochures for information? Thank you very much in advance. I'm looking forward to your answer. My family and I can't wait to start our "Harry Potter tour".

Yours faithfully,

...

2. Picture-based Writing: Picture and Prompts (Einzelbild und Impulse)

Hinweis: Betrachte zunächst die Abbildung genau. Dann kannst du überlegen, wie du die Stichpunkte sinnvoll in deinen Text einbauen kannst. Beziehe auch die Informationen aus dem Bild mit ein. Anhand der Poster kannst du z. B. sehen, dass Alex u. a. ein Fußballfan ist.

A Dream Comes True

One rainy afternoon Alex Andersen (aged 21) was reading his brand-new Harry Potter book when he fell asleep. He had a wonderful dream ...

Alex dreamed that Harry Potter came flying into his room. "That's Harry Potter! I can't believe it!", Alex cried out. "Yes, it's me.", Harry said. "You have one wish. Tell me what you like to have." Alex didn't think long about that. "I would like to have so much money that I can buy everything." So Harry took his wand, said some magic spells and suddenly thousands of bank notes came out of his wand.

Alex couldn't believe his eyes. He was happy because now he could buy whatever he liked. He could get one of the best seats to watch a football match, for example. He could also drive in a racing car like Michael Schumacher, or see his favourite band as often as he liked. Suddenly, he woke up and realized that this was only a dream.

Alex was a bit disappointed but then his mother came in with a letter from the national lottery. Now he really couldn't believe his eyes. He was the winner of last week's lottery! So his dream has finally come true.

Notenschlüssel

Notenstufen	1	2	3	4	5	6
Punkte	70 – 61,5	61,0 – 50,5	50,0 – 37,5	37,0 – 22,5	22,0 – 11,5	11,0 – 0

A Listening

Allgemeiner Hinweis: Die Dialoge werden von einer CD abgespielt. Beantworte die zugehörigen Aufgaben. Rechtschreibfehler werden in diesem Prüfungsteil nicht bewertet.

Tapescript 1: Sam is talking to his boss Mrs Smith.

1 SAM: You wanted to see me?

MRS SMITH: Yes, ... You know, Sam. During your three weeks' work experience at our hospital, you really did a great job. And you also have good grades in school. But there is a problem.

5 SAM: What is it?

MRS SMITH: Well, Sam, some patients have complained about your tattoo.

SAM: But it's only a little dragon on my hand!

MRS SMITH: Actually, it's quite a large dragon. It gives our patients the wrong impression of you.

10 SAM: Really?

MRS SMITH: Yes, many patients really don't like your tattoo. It makes them feel uncomfortable and they are a bit afraid of you.

SAM: Do you mean I have no chance of getting a job here? I really hoped I could work here after I finished school.

15 MRS SMITH: I'm sorry, Sam, but with this tattoo, we simply can't give you a job.

1. hospital
   Hinweis: Z. 2f.

2. grades
   Hinweis: Z. 3f.

3. tattoo
   Hinweis: Z. 6

4. afraid
   Hinweis: Z. 11f.

Tapescript 2: After work Sam meets his friend, Megan.

1 MEGAN: What's wrong, Sam?

SAM: Well, you know how excited I was about my work experience at the hospital. It's a really great place to work.

MEGAN: Yes, you told me. Oh, maybe they will offer you a job after you finish school.

5 SAM: No, they don't want me. It's because of my tattoo.

MEGAN: What! Well, you can get it removed.

SAM: But that's difficult.

MEGAN: Oh, no, I heard it's very easy. You can just use a cream to remove tattoos.

SAM: But this tattoo is permanent. When I got it my parents had to give their

10 permission. And at first my mom didn't want to sign the piece of paper.

MEGAN: Well, let's look on the internet and see if we can find some tattoo removal cream for you.

SAM: Maybe I should call my doctor first. What do you think?

1 great
   Hinweis: *Z. 3*

2 job
   Hinweis: *Z. 4*

3 mom
   Hinweis: *Z. 10*

4 doctor
   Hinweis: *Z. 13*

Tapescript 3: Sam talks to his doctor.

1 DOCTOR: So, young man. What can I do for you?

SAM: Well, ah, … I have a tattoo and I don't want it anymore. My friend told me about a cream that removes tattoos. Can you tell me if it works?

DOCTOR: A cream is not a good idea. I wouldn't use it.

5 SAM: What should I do then?

DOCTOR: Well, the easiest thing to do is to cover it with your clothing. Wear long sleeves.

SAM: No, I would have to wear gloves to cover it. Look here, it's on my hand.

DOCTOR: Oh, it's going to be a problem. Tattoos are very difficult to remove.

10 Laser treatment is best but that's expensive and it can take up to a year for the tattoo to disappear.

SAM: And will it go away completely?

DOCTOR: Sometimes. But I'm sorry to say that you might always have some
colour left in your skin. It has green, red or yellow in it, doesn't it?

5 SAM: Yes. the dragon is green, the eyes are red and the tail is yellow.

DOCTOR: Well, unfortunately, red, green and yellow inks tend to leave a mark
that will not go away.

SAM: Oh, dear, that doesn't sound good.

DOCTOR: Look, why don't you speak to your parents and see what they think.

10 SAM: Ok, I'll do that. Thank you.

1. True
   Hinweis: Z. 2 f.

2. False
   Hinweis: Z. 4

3. False
   Hinweis: Z. 6 ff.

4. True
   Hinweis: Z. 10 f.

5. False
   Hinweis: Z. 13

6. False
   Hinweis: Z. 15

7. True
   Hinweis: Z. 16 f.

8. True
   Hinweis: Z. 19

Tapescript 4: Sam is talking to his mother on the way to the doctor.

1 MOM: Oh Sam, I never wanted you to get that tattoo! This is going to be painful
and expensive. I'll pay the $ 200 for your first treatment but you're going to
pay for the rest.

SAM: But Mom, I'll need at least five more treatments! That'll cost $ 1,000!

5 MOM: Don't complain! You wanted that tattoo! I just hope you learn your lesson.

SAM: I've heard it hurts, Mom. I'm a little bit scared.

MOM: Don't worry, you'll be fine. By the way, I'm glad that the job at the hospital
is more important to you than your tattoo.

1. $ 300
   Hinweis: „ $ 200" (Z. 2 f.)
2. four
   Hinweis: „five" (Z. 4)
3. sad
   Hinweis: „scared" (Z. 6)
4. happy
   Hinweis: „glad" (Z. 7)

B Use of English

Hinweis: In diesem Prüfungsteil darfst du <u>kein</u> Wörterbuch verwenden. Solltest du Rechtschreibfehler machen, die das Wort so verändern, dass man den Inhalt oder den Sinn nicht mehr versteht, verlierst du Punkte.

Aufgabe 1

Hinweis: Streiche pro Zeile nur das eine falsche Wort, das nicht zu den anderen passt. Falls du mehrere Wörter streichst, erhältst du auf die gesamte Teilaufgabe keine Punkte.

a) bill
   Hinweis: Vokabeln zum Wortfeld „Bewerbung":
   application – Bewerbung
   CV – Lebenslauf
   interview – Vorstellungsgespräch

b) handy
   Hinweis: Vokabeln zum Wortfeld „Telefon":
   cellphone / mobile – Mobiltelefon, Handy;
   „handy" wird im englischen Sprachgebrauch nicht verwendet!

c) map
   Hinweis: Vokabeln zum Wortfeld „Restaurant":
   menu – Speisekarte
   order – Bestellung
   starter – Vorspeise

Aufgabe 2

Hinweis: *Falls du Legastheniker/in bist, musst du diese Aufgabe nicht bearbeiten. Die korrekte Schreibweise der Wörter ist in Klammern angegeben.*

Hi Mike,

~~Mai~~ (My) name is Robert. I'm twelve ~~jears~~ (years) old and I live in ~~bavaria~~ (Bavaria). I've got a brother. He's older ~~then~~ (than) me. He likes sports, but I ~~prifer~~ (prefer) computer games. Next week ~~i~~ (I) will get an MP3-player. That's ~~graet~~ (great)! ~~Waht~~ (What) about you? Please write soon.

Yours,
Robert

Aufgabe 3

Usually we meet ~~at~~ my uncle's house ~~on~~ Sundays. ~~At~~ /~~Around~~ /~~Before~~ 5 o'clock ~~in~~ the afternoon we always have a cup ~~of~~ coffee. Uncle Sam's dog sleeps ~~under~~ / ~~beside~~ /~~beneath~~ /~~next to~~ /~~near~~ the table. We go home ~~after~~ /~~for~~ /~~before~~ dinner.

Aufgabe 4

a) Have you already got your new tattoo? / Have you got your new tattoo already?

Hinweis: *Der Fragesatz beginnt mit dem Hilfsverb „have".*

b) Last week I had an appointment. / I had an appointment last week.

Hinweis: *appointment – Termin*
Die Zeitangabe „last week" kann im Aussagesatz am Satzanfang oder am Satzende stehen.

c) Protect it from the sun!

Hinweis: *Bei einer Aufforderung steht das Verb, hier „protect", am Satzanfang.*

Aufgabe 5

Birgit <u>went</u> to Australia in 2005.

Hinweis: Die Zeitangabe „in 2005" zeigt an, dass das Verb in das simple past gesetzt werden muss.

She <u>left</u> Germany with her parents.

Hinweis: Auch dieser Satz bezieht sich noch auf das Jahr 2005.

Two months ago, Birgit <u>started</u> a new job at the supermarket.

Hinweis: Die Zeitangabe „two months ago" zeigt an, dass das Verb im simple past stehen muss.

She really <u>enjoys</u> working there.

Hinweis: Hier musst du das simple present einsetzen, da Birgit immer noch in dem Supermarkt arbeitet und es ihr dort gefällt.

Her parents <u>don't like</u> the house they live in.

Hinweis: Auch in diesem Satz muss eine Gegenwartsform verwendet werden. Im nächsten Satz wird klar, warum hier keine Vergangenheitsform stehen kann.

So they <u>will move</u> /<u>are moving</u> /<u>are going to move</u> into a big farmhouse next month.

Hinweis: Die Zeitangabe „next month" zeigt an, dass das Verb in einer Zukunfts-Form stehen muss.

Aufgabe 6

Robert: <u>Where</u> did you learn English?

Birgit: At a school in London.

Robert: <u>When</u> did you arrive in Australia?

Birgit: I arrived in 2005.

Robert: <u>Who</u> came with you?

Birgit: My parents.

Robert: <u>How</u> did you travel?

Birgit: I travelled by plane.

Robert: <u>Why</u> did you choose Australia?

Birgit: I chose Australia, because I love the warm climate.

Robert: <u>Where</u> do your parents originally come from?

Birgit: They come from Europe.

Robert: <u>What</u> are your plans for the future?

Birgit: I'd like to buy a farm in the outback.

Aufgabe 7

Hinweis: *allow sb./sth. to do sth. – jmd./etw. erlauben etw. zu tun*
never mind – kein Problem, „macht nichts"

1	2	3	4	5
e	a	b	f	d

C Reading

Allgemeiner Hinweis: *In diesem Prüfungsteil darfst du ein zweisprachiges Wörterbuch benutzen.*

Vokabelhinweise:

Z. 6	*to admire – bewundern*
Z. 15	*reminder – eine Erinnerung an*
Z. 17	*taste – Geschmack*
Z. 19	*to increase – steigern*
Z. 26	*to express – ausdrücken*
Z. 29	*to refer to – sich beziehen auf*
Z. 35	*to point out – darauf hinweisen, deutlich machen*
Z. 41	*in addition to – zusätzlich*
Z. 49	*to swallow – schlucken*
Z. 50	*to include – beinhalten*
Z. 53	*life-threatening – lebensgefährlich*
Z. 55	*health precautions – Gesundheitsvorkehrungen*
Z. 64	*relationship – Beziehung*
Z. 68	*temporary – vorübergehend, zeitlich begrenzt*
Z. 70	*to remove – entfernen*

Aufgabe 1

A	B	C	D
3	4	2	1

Hinweis: *permanent – dauerhaft*
temporary – vorübergehend

Aufgabe 2

Hinweis: *Wenn du Rechtschreibfehler machst, die dazu führen, dass man den Sinn des Wortes nicht mehr versteht, verlierst du Punkte.*

a) Piercings and tattoos

b) I dress this way to shock you.

c) Infections, Aids, Hepatitis B, cracks or broken teeth, damage to nerves, allergic reactions, long healing time

d) Using new latex gloves and new needles for each customer.

e) They only last for a few days or even a week. You can remove them easily. You can enjoy the fun of "body art" with a new design whenever you like, without any risk.

Aufgabe 3

	True	False	Not in the text
a) Some people get a tattoo to attract a new partner.	✓		
b) Tattoos are not allowed at school.			✓
c) Jonathan has got 10 piercings all over his body.		✓	
d) Most doctors say that tattoos and piercings are no problem.		✓	
e) Health problems caused by body art are not paid by health insurance.			✓
f) A piercing through the tongue can damage nerves.	✓		

Aufgabe 4

Which lines from the text tell you ...	lines
a) ... that some people get a tattoo to remember something special in their lives?	15–16
b) ... that piercings can take up to a year to heal?	39–41
c) ... that removing tattoos hurts and costs a lot of money?	66–67

D Text Production

Allgemeiner Hinweis: *Auch in diesem Prüfungsteil darfst du ein zweisprachiges Wörterbuch verwenden. Entscheide dich bei der Bearbeitung <u>entweder</u> für die Email <u>oder</u> für die Bildergeschichte.*

1. Correspondence: E-Mail

Hinweis: In der Aufgabenstellung findest du Hinweise zum Inhalt der E-mail. Baue möglichst viele dieser Inhalte in deinen Text ein. Wenn du willst, kannst du diese Vorgaben auch teilweise durch eigene Ideen ergänzen oder ersetzen. Wichtig ist, dass der Umfang der E-mail mindestens 10 Sätze beträgt. Achte beim Schreiben der E-mail auch darauf, dass du den Empfänger begrüßt und dich am Ende von ihm verabschiedest.

Hello Chris,

Thanks for your mail. I haven't finished my exams yet. My last exam is one week before I come to see you in Liverpool. I'm very happy that we'll meet during the holidays.

It's a great idea to go to London together! We can visit some interesting places and maybe we can go to a concert in the city. I'm also looking forward to seeing Buckingham Palace.

It's cool that you got a tattoo. Did it hurt? I am curious to see what it shows. Could you send me a photo?

Please write back soon!

Bye,

Michael

2. Picture-based Writing:

Hinweis: Bevor du mit dem Schreiben beginnst, solltest du die Abbildungen genau betrachten. Finde den Höhepunkt der Geschichte heraus (Ians bester Freund ist sein Hund Rocky) und überlege dir weitere Punkte, die für das Verständnis der Bilderge-schichte wichtig sind (Angebot im Schaufenster des Friseurs, Rockys neuer Haar-schnitt, Ians Reaktion auf das Aussehen seines Hundes). Verfasse anschließend einen Text, der die gesamte Bildergeschichte erzählt. Denke daran, auch die wörtliche Rede zu verwenden.

One Saturday morning Ian Carpenter was taking his dog Rocky for a walk. On his way to the park, he passed a hairdresser's shop. There was a poster in the shop window. It said: *Get a new hairstyle. Your best friend is free!* Both Ian and his dog Rocky had very long hair.

So they went inside the shop and Ian told Julian and Lucy, the hairdressers, that he wanted to take the offer[1]. "But where's your best friend?" the hairdressers asked. "He's right there!" Ian answered and pointed to his dog Rocky.

"Please cut the dog's hair," Julian told Lucy. Lucy was not happy about this job. She took Rocky to a part of the room that was hidden[2] behind a curtain. While Julian was styling Ian, Lucy was busy with Rocky.

When Julian had finished, Ian checked himself in the mirror. He liked his new hairstyle and paid Julian for it. "What about Rocky?" Ian asked. Lucy opened the curtain and brought Rocky. The dog had almost no hair left and looked like he was styled for the circus. Ian was really shocked about the dog's new look!

1 offer – Angebot
2 to hide – verbergen

Notenschlüssel

Notenstufen	1	2	3	4	5	6
Punkte	70–61	60,5–50	49,5–36	35,5–22	21,5–11	10,5–0

Notenschlüssel für Legastheniker

Notenstufen	1	2	3	4	5	6
Punkte	66,5–59,5	59–48,5	48–34,5	34–21,5	21–10	9,5–0

A Listening

Allgemeiner Hinweis: *Die folgenden Dialoge hörst du immer je zweimal. Höre genau auf die Anweisungen und versuche, die Aufgaben zu lösen. Sieh dir den Text erst an, wenn du nicht mehr weiterkommst.*

Tapescript 1

FATHER: What's the matter, Mary? Is everything OK? You don't look very happy.

MARY: Oh, Dad, I don't know what to do.

FATHER: What do you mean?

MARY: This morning as I was walking past some of my friends outside school, they all started laughing. I felt like they were laughing at me.

FATHER: What did you do then?

MARY: Oh, I just walked away.

FATHER: Mmm.

MARY: And the other thing is ... well, I've been getting some really horrible emails recently. I can't see who they're from because I don't recognise the addresses.

FATHER: Oh, no.

MARY: But whoever the people are, they're saying horrible things about me. You know, things that aren't true at all.

FATHER: Think for a moment. I mean, maybe you've said something to somebody at school and made them angry.

MARY: Well, I did have an argument with Susan last week.

FATHER: OK.

MARY: And I know she's still angry with me, because she hasn't spoken to me since then.

FATHER: But would Susan send you horrible emails?

MARY: No, no ...well ... I don't think so.

FATHER: OK. Look. When you tell me you are receiving horrible emails, it sounds to me – well –, as if it could be cyber bullying or something like that. I think we should phone the police.

MARY: The police?

FATHER: Yes, they have a special helpline for information about cyber bullying. They can tell us what to do.

1. a) laughed at her
   Hinweis: *Z. 5*

2. c) walked away
   Hinweis: *Z. 7*

3. b) Last week
   Hinweis: *Z. 17*

4. c) what to do
   Hinweis: *Z. 28*

5. b) Friends
   Hinweis: *Z. 4 f.; 17*

Tapescript 2

1　POLICE: Hello. What can I do for you?
　MARY: Well, um ... I've got a big problem. I don't think I can solve it on my own.
　POLICE: OK. Can you tell me what it is?
　MARY: Yes, people are sending me nasty emails.
5　POLICE: Oh ...
　MARY: And lies about my private life are being posted on the internet.
　POLICE: I see. And how are things at school at the moment?
　MARY: Well, nobody in my class talks to me. They all ignore me.
　POLICE: I see ... Have you had an argument with anybody recently?
10　MARY: Yeah. Last week I had a big fight with my best friend.
　POLICE: And what's your friend's name?
　MARY: Susan. But she's not my friend anymore.
　POLICE: Susan. And she's in your class, you said.
　MARY: Yes.
15　POLICE: Right. Now, the first thing you should do is to speak to your parents about what's going on.
　MARY: Yes. In fact it was my Dad's idea that I contact you.
　POLICE: Good. Next point: do not open any emails from people you don't know.
　MARY: Oh, OK. I never thought of that.
20　POLICE: And the last thing ...
　MARY: Yes?
　POLICE: Save all the nasty messages you get.
　MARY: Save them? Why?
　POLICE: Well, any nasty messages you receive will help us to find out who's be-
25　hind this problem.
　MARY: I understand. OK. Great. Thanks for your help.

1. False
   Hinweis: *Z. 2*
2. True
   Hinweis: *Z. 6*
3. False
   Hinweis: *Z. 12*
4. True
   Hinweis: *Z. 15 f.*
5. False
   Hinweis: *Z. 18*
6. True
   Hinweis: *Z. 22*

Tapescript 3

POLICE: Hello Susan.

SUSAN: Hello.

POLICE: Please come in and have a seat.

SUSAN: Thank you.

POLICE: Now, do you know why I wanted to talk to you today?

SUSAN: No, not really.

POLICE: It's about your friend, Mary.

SUSAN: Mary?

POLICE: Yes. Mary told us you two were best friends and she trusted you.

SUSAN: Yes.

POLICE: And she also told us that she gave you the password for her email account. Is that true?

SUSAN: Um ... yes, it is.

POLICE: And is it true that you used Mary's account to send nasty emails to Mary's friends?

SUSAN: Er ...

POLICE: And that Mary's friends thought <u>Mary</u> had sent those emails?

SUSAN: But it was only a joke! Honestly! Mary and I had an argument and I was ... I was really angry with her!

POLICE: But using Mary's email account isn't a joke! It's a serious matter, Susan. Do you know what it's called?

SUSAN: No.

POLICE: Cyber bullying.

1. ~~good~~: best
   / Hinweis: Z. 9
2. ~~nice~~: nasty
   / Hinweis: Z. 14 f.
3. ~~internet~~: email
   / Hinweis: Z. 20

B Use of English

/ **Hinweis:** *Anhand der folgenden Aufgaben werden dein Wortschatz, deine Gram-*
/ *matik-Kenntnisse und deine Ausdrucksfähigkeit in kommunikativen Situationen be-*
/ *urteilt. In diesem Prüfungsteil darfst du* <u>kein</u> *Wörterbuch benutzen.*

Aufgabe 1

/ **Hinweis:** *Hier musst du die gegenteilige Bedeutung des unterstrichenen Wortes auf*
/ *Englisch einsetzen. Es kann dir helfen, wenn du das unterstrichene Wort ins Deut-*
/ *sche übersetzt. Achte auch auf den Satzzusammenhang.*

a) You enter the cinema through the <u>entrance</u> and you leave it through the <u>exit</u>.
   / **Hinweis:** entrance: *Eingang; Ausgang:* exit

b) Peter can't <u>spend</u> all his money. He wants to buy a new MP3-player, so he must <u>save</u> at least € 5 a month.
   / **Hinweis:** to spend: *(Geld) ausgeben; sparen:* to save

c) I <u>go to bed</u> at 8 p.m. when I have to <u>get up</u> early next morning.
   / **Hinweis:** to go to bed: *Schlafen gehen; aufstehen:* to get up

d) Spending your holiday at home is usually very <u>cheap</u>, but going to another country can be quite <u>expensive</u>.
   / **Hinweis:** cheap: *preiswert; teuer:* expensive

Aufgabe 2

a) I am sure that we <u>will</u> visit New York next year, because we all <u>want to</u> see the Statue of Liberty.
   / **Hinweis:** *Das Signalwort „next year" weist auf die Verwendung der Zukunfts-*
   / *form „will" hin. In der nächsten Lücke macht nur „want to" (wollen) Sinn.*
   / *„Would" (würde) ergibt im Satzzusammenhang keinen Sinn.*

b) The new movie is really <u>interesting</u>. Everybody is <u>interested in</u> it.
   Hinweis: interesting: *interessant;* to be interested in sth.: *sich für etw. interessieren;* interest: *das Interesse*

Aufgabe 3

Hinweis: *Spreche dir, wenn du zu Hause übst, die einzelnen Wörter laut vor, dann fallen dir die Unterschiede in der Aussprache leichter auf.*

a) wait   b) long   c) cute   d) friend

Aufgabe 4

Hinweis: *Hier geht es darum, dass du erkennst, ob du ein Adjektiv oder ein Adverb einsetzen musst.*

a) Jane is an <u>attractive</u> girl, but she sings <u>terribly</u>.
   Hinweis: attractive *(Adjektiv);* terribly: *furchtbar (Die Endung -ly zeigt, dass es sich um ein Adverb handelt: Auf welche Art und Weise singt Jane?:* terribly)

b) Mike is one of the <u>best</u> players on his football team.
   Hinweis: one of the best: *einer der besten*

c) When all the students work <u>carefully/well</u> the teacher is really <u>happy</u>.
   Hinweis: *Adverbien:* carefully: *gewissenhaft;* well: *gut; Adjektiv:* happy: *glücklich/zufrieden (Wie ist der Lehrer/die Lehrerin?:* happy)

Aufgabe 5

Hinweis: *Hier musst du jeweils das richtige persönliche Fürwort* (I, you, he/she/it, we, you, they) *oder besitzanzeigende Fürwort* (my, your, his/her/its, our, your, their) *eintragen. Achte auf die vorangehenden Sätze, dann kannst aus dem Sinn erschließen, welches Fürwort du einsetzen musst. Auch gibt dir das Verb einen Hinweis: eine Form mit der Endung -s bedeutet, dass du als persönliches Fürwort nur* he, she *oder* it *verwenden kannst, z.B. in* "She works in a hospital".

Peter is 15 years old. <u>His</u> older brother is 17 years old. <u>They</u> live together with <u>their</u> parents in a nice little house. <u>Their</u> mother is a nurse. <u>She</u> works in a hospital. Peter's father works for an international company. <u>He</u> really loves his job and always says, "I love <u>my</u> job because <u>I</u> can meet people from all over the world."

Aufgabe 6

Hinweis: Hier geht es darum, If-Sätze vom Typ I zu vervollständigen. Dabei musst du darauf achten, dass im Hauptsatz will + die Grundform des Verbs und im Nebensatz if + die simple present-Form des Verbs steht.

a) If we go to South Africa we <u>will</u> visit a national park.

b) If my father <u>lends</u> me his camera, I will be able to take really good photos.

c) I <u>will be</u> very happy, if we can go to my friend's birthday party.

Aufgabe 7

Hinweis: Hier sollst du die richtige Zeitform des Verbs einsetzen. In Klammern ist jeweils der Name der Zeitform angegeben, sodass du sie in der Kurzgrammatik schnell findest. Achte auch auf die Signalwörter. Sie sind in der Lösung fett markiert.

John <u>has played</u> *(present perfect)* / <u>has been</u> playing *(present perfect progressive)* computer games with his friends **for years**. They **usually** <u>meet</u> *(simple present)* at a club. It's the same club where John <u>works</u> *(simple present)* **every weekend**. **Yesterday** some of the club members <u>found</u> *(simple past)* bad messages on the net. **At the moment**, they <u>are</u> talking *(present progressive)* to a police officer. The police officer <u>will</u> come *(will-future)* / <u>is</u> going to come *(going to-future)* to their school **next week**.

Aufgabe 8

Hinweis: Hier musst du einen Dialog vervollständigen, wie er im Alltag vorkommen kann. Du kannst wählen, ob du ein single ticket (Ticket nur für die Hinfahrt), oder ein return ticket (Ticket für die Hin- und Rückfahrt) kaufen möchtest.

TICKET ASSISTANT: Good afternoon! How can I help you?

YOU: Good afternoon. <u>I'd like to go</u> / <u>I'd like a ticket</u> to Canberra.

TICKET ASSISTANT: Single or return?

YOU: <u>Single</u> / <u>Return</u> please. <u>How much</u> is the ticket?

TICKET ASSISTANT: That will be $ 48. Here's your ticket.

YOU: Thank you. <u>When does (will) the train arrive</u> in Canberra?

TICKET ASSISTANT: It arrives at 10 o'clock.

YOU: <u>Where does</u> / <u>From which</u> <u>platform does</u> the train leave?

TICKET ASSISTANT: From platform 7.

YOU: Thanks very much.

TICKET ASSISTANT: You're welcome. Have a nice trip.

C Reading

Allgemeiner Hinweis: *In diesem Prüfungsteil darfst du ein zweisprachiges Wörter-buch benutzen.*

Vokabelhinweise:

Z. 3	*message* – Botschaft
Z. 5	*BC (before Christ)* – vor Christus
Z. 7	*progress* – Fortschritt
Z. 9	*development* – Entwicklung
Z. 16	*inventor* – Erfinder
Z. 27 f.	*soon after* – kurz darauf
Z. 52	*to increase* – erhöhen
Z. 65	*influence* – Einfluss
Z. 65 f.	*development* – Entwicklung

Aufgabe 1

a) ... the Chinese government.
  Hinweis: *Z. 5 ff.*

b) ... 50 years.
  Hinweis: *Z. 31 ff.*

c) ... it was only possible between computers of the same network.
  Hinweis: *Z. 38 ff.*

d) ... use of @ in emails.
  Hinweis: *Z. 45 ff.*

Aufgabe 2

Hinweis: *Lies für diese Aufgabe den Text noch einmal ganz durch, um danach die angegebenen Fakten in die richtige Reihenfolge zu bringen.*

1	e
2	b
3	g
4	f
5	d
6	c
7	a

Aufgabe 3

Hinweis: *Lies den Text noch einmal und beantworte die Fragen in Stichpunkten.*

a) by runners and later by messengers on horseback
  Hinweis: Z. 3 f

b) Mr Watson / his assistant
  Hinweis: Z. 22 f.

c) the (telephone) answering machine
  Hinweis: Z. 27 ff.

d) Neil Papworth
  Hinweis: Z. 59 ff.

e) teenagers
  Hinweis: Z. 64 ff.

f) L8R
  Hinweis: Z. 73 f.

D Text Production

Allgemeiner Hinweis: *Auch in diesem Prüfungsteil darfst du ein zweisprachiges Wörterbuch verwenden. Entscheide dich bei der Bearbeitung <u>entweder</u> für die Email <u>oder</u> für die Bildergeschichte.*

1. Correspondence: E-Mail

Hinweis: *In der Aufgabenstellung findest du Vorgaben zum Inhalt der E-mail. Baue möglichst alle Vorgaben in deinen Text ein. Du kannst auch eigene Ideen hinzufügen. Wichtig ist, dass der Umfang der E-mail mindestens 10 Sätze (mindestens 80 Wörter) beträgt und in sich schlüssig ist. Beachte, dass es sich hier um eine Bewerbung handelt und du somit nicht in der Umgangssprache schreiben kannst. Achte beim Schreiben der E-mail auch darauf, dass du den Empfänger begrüßt und dich am Ende von ihm verabschiedest. Der Empfänger ist in diesem Fall eine Frau. Da du nicht weißt, ob Frau Byrd verheiratet ist (Mrs) oder nicht (Miss), musst du die neutrale Anrede (Ms) benutzen.*

Vokabelhinweise:
hours – hier: Geschäftszeiten, Arbeitszeiten
location – Ort
duration – Dauer
temporary – zeitlich begrenzt
description – Beschreibung
skills required – erforderliche Fähigkeiten
how to apply – „wie man sich bewirbt" = Bewerbungsverfahren
employer – Arbeitgeber

Dear Ms Byrd,

I found your summer job offer on the ROBIN HOOD CLUBS web page.

My name is Daniel Wagner, and I am a 15-year-old student from Bamberg, Germany. I am interested in helping the child minder at Robin Hood Clubs in Kyllini, because I would like to have a summer job that makes it possible for me to work with children and practise my English. I am also a great fan of Greece, where I have already been on holiday with my parents.

I am used to looking after children because I have two younger sisters, aged 7 and 5. I often take care of them in the afternoons because both my parents work.

I like sports very much. I am a member of my school's swimming team, and I often play badminton with my friends. The languages I speak are German and English.

Could you please send me some information about how much I would earn and about where I would stay while working at Robin Hood Clubs?

I have attached my photo and CV to this mail, and I am looking forward to hearing from you.

Yours sincerely,
Daniel Wagner

2. Picture-based Writing:

Hinweis: Bevor du mit dem Schreiben beginnst, solltest du die Abbildungen genau betrachten. Berücksichtige beim Schreiben die inhaltlichen Vorgaben.

Last September the Huber family planned a trip to South Africa. They found a lot of information about Kruger National Park on the internet and they booked their holiday, including a trip to the park.

During the Christmas holiday 2009, the Hubers started their guided day trip to Kruger National Park. They were all very excited and hoped that they would see some wild animals.

Soon after they had gone into the park, their tour truck had a flat tyre. When the tour guide, who was also the driver, was changing the wheel, little Annika Huber saw a lion coming towards them and started to scream. Everybody quickly fled into the driver's cabin of the truck. Now the lion was right in front of the truck and waited. Annika's brother Tim was very scared and thought they would all die. But after some minutes, the lion just went away. The Hubers were very happy because the lion wasn't hungry that day!

Notenschlüssel

Notenstufen	1	2	3	4	5	6
Punkte	68–60	59,5–49	48,5–37	36,5–22	21,5–12	11,5–0

A Listening

Allgemeiner Hinweis: *Die folgenden Dialoge hörst du je zweimal. Achte genau auf die Anweisungen. Versuche, die Aufgaben selbstständig zu lösen und sieh die Lösungen erst nach Bearbeitung der Aufgaben an.*

Part 1

JENNY: Hello. Um. ... Heathrow Airport, please.
TAXI DRIVER: Heathrow? OK. Where are you flying to?
JENNY: Sorry?
TAXI DRIVER: Which terminal is it?
JENNY: It's terminal ... um ... wait a second ... one, I think. To Munich.
TAXI DRIVER: OK. Which airline did you say?
JENNY: British Airways. At 11.30.
TAXI DRIVER: British Airways? Ah, that's terminal 5.
JENNY: Really?
TAXI DRIVER: Yeah, all British Airways flights go from there.
JENNY: Let me check. Um. Yeah, yeah. You're right.
(Taxi hält an.)
TAXI DRIVER: OK. Here we are. That's £ 23.50, please.
JENNY: Thank you.
TAXI DRIVER: Oh, thanks. Do you need any help with your bags?
JENNY: That'd be lovely. They're quite heavy.
TAXI DRIVER: OK. You grab a trolley and I'll get everything out of the boot.
JENNY: Thanks.
TAXI DRIVER: There you are. When did you say your flight was?
JENNY: 11.30.
TAXI DRIVER: Oh, you'd better hurry then. It's quarter to eleven already.
JENNY: Really? 10.45. Oh no!

1. 11.30
   Hinweis: Z. 7
2. 5
   Hinweis: Z. 8
3. £ 23.50
   Hinweis: Z. 13

4. 10.45
Hinweis: Z. 22

Part 2

1 JENNY: Hello.
MAN FROM BA: Hello there.
JENNY: I'm booked on the 11.30 flight to Munich but I haven't been able to check in yet.
5 MAN FROM BA: That's OK. Can I have your passport, please? Thanks. How many items of luggage are you checking in? Two?
JENNY: No, just this big suitcase.
MAN FROM BA: OK. And that bag? Is that your hand luggage?
JENNY: That's right. I'm not too late, am I?
10 MAN FROM BA: No, no. Can you put the suitcase on the scales, please?
JENNY: It's quite heavy, but I hope it's not ... too heavy.
MAN FROM BA: Hmm ... seventeen kilos. That's fine. The weight limit is 23.
JENNY: Oh, good. Do you think I could have a window seat?
MAN FROM BA: Let me have a look. Um. No, I'm afraid that's not going to work.
15 And there are no aisle seats left either.
JENNY: Oh, OK.
MAN FROM BA: Sorry about that. So, that's 16 B.
JENNY: 16 B. OK. Thanks.
MAN FROM BA: Boarding begins at five past eleven so you've got 10 minutes.
20 JENNY: Great. Thanks.
MAN FROM BA: Gate 15.
JENNY: OK. Is that far to walk?
MAN FROM BA: No, no, it's very close. You can see it from here.

1. a bag and a suitcase.
Hinweis: Z. 7–9

2. 17 kilos.
Hinweis: Z. 12

3. a middle seat.
Hinweis: Z. 13–15

Part 3

VOICE: Good morning, ladies and gentlemen. This is an important announcement for passengers checked in on flight BA 942 to Munich. This flight is scheduled to leave at 11.30. Because of a problem we are having with the onboard computer system there will be a short delay. We apologise for this situation. You will understand that our engineers are doing everything they can to make sure the flight leaves as soon as possible. We would ask all passengers to stay near the gate and wait for further announcements. We hope to give you an update in the next ten to fifteen minutes. Once again, we apologise for the delay.

1. This is an important announcement for passengers ~~booked~~ in on flight BA 942 to Munich.
   Hinweis: Z. 2 *(checked in)*

2. Because of a problem we are having with the onboard computer system there will be a ~~small~~ delay.
   Hinweis: Z. 4 *(short)*

3. You will understand that our ~~pilots~~ are doing everything they can to make sure the flight leaves as soon as possible.
   Hinweis: Z. 5 *(engineers)*

4. We would ask all passengers to ~~sit~~ near the gate and wait for further announcements.
   Hinweis: Z. 6 *(stay)*

Part 4

YOUNG WOMAN: Hey, are you also waiting for the flight to Munich?
JENNY: Yeah.
YOUNG WOMAN: Have you been on holiday here?
JENNY: No, no. I was doing a language course, in Brighton.
YOUNG WOMAN: Oh, Brighton! I know Brighton well. And did you enjoy it?
JENNY: Yeah, it was excellent. And I was staying with a family there. They were great, too.
YOUNG WOMAN: Oh, so it was quite intensive then. One week, did you say?
JENNY: No, two weeks. And yesterday I was in London, in Brixton ...
YOUNG WOMAN: Brixton. OK.
JENNY: ... visiting some friends and doing some shopping.
YOUNG WOMAN: Lovely.
JENNY: And last night we all went to a musical ...
YOUNG WOMAN: OK.

15 JENNY: And then in the evening when we got back I forgot to set my alarm clock ...
YOUNG WOMAN: Oh dear.
JENNY: ... and this morning I missed the train.
YOUNG WOMAN: Oh no.
JENNY: So I had no time for breakfast and had to get a taxi instead.
20 YOUNG WOMAN: Well, you made it.
JENNY: Yeah. The taxi was expensive, but the driver was really friendly.
(Pause)
YOUNG WOMAN: Look, would you like a cup of coffee?
JENNY: That's a good idea. I need to eat something as well.
25 YOUNG WOMAN: Shall we go over there to that café?
(Jingle)
JENNY: Wait a second. That could be for us.
YOUNG WOMAN: Oh no. Not another delay!
VOICE: Thank you for being so patient, ladies and gentlemen. BA 942 to Munich
30 is now ready for boarding. Please have your passport *(fade out)* and boarding
   card ready when you come forward to the gate. Thank you again. We wish you
   a pleasant flight.

1. False
   Hinweis: Z. 4 *("I was doing a language course ...")*
2. False
   Hinweis: Z. 6 *("... I was staying with a family there.")*
3. True
   Hinweis: Z. 9
4. False
   Hinweis: Z. 13 *("... we all went to a musical.")*
5. False
   Hinweis: Z. 15 *("... in the evening ... I forgot to set my alarm clock.")*
6. True
   Hinweis: Z. 19
7. True
   Hinweis: Z. 21
8. True
   Hinweis: Z. 25 ff.

B Use of English

Aufgabe 1

Every day I <u>turn on</u> my computer. Sometimes I <u>need</u> it for my homework because we often have to <u>write</u> texts. Once I lost an important text so now I always <u>save</u> everything immediately. There are also a lot of photos on my computer. I <u>send</u> the nicest ones to my friends.

Aufgabe 2

a) menu   b) bill

c) kitchen   d) knife

Aufgabe 3

a) there – pair

b) own – stone

c) said – bread

d) why – pie

Aufgabe 4

London is the <u>biggest</u> city in England. The London Underground is the <u>oldest</u> underground system in the world. People use it because it is <u>faster</u> than the buses. Taking a taxi is <u>more expensive</u> than using public transport. One of the <u>best</u> ways to get around the centre of London is on foot.

Aufgabe 5

Hinweis: *Wähle jeweils das passende Verb aus und setze es in die* simple past-*Form.*
Zu Formen und Verwendung des simple past *siehe S. 92 in deiner Kurzgrammatik.*

Yesterday Susan <u>met</u> her friend Beth in town. First the girls <u>went</u> to a café and <u>had</u> a milkshake. Then they <u>did</u> some shopping. They <u>spent</u> an hour in a clothes shop but they <u>didn't buy</u> anything. Later they <u>watched</u> an interesting film at the cinema.

Aufgabe 6

Hinweis: *Hier musst du jeweils die richtige Antwort oder Reaktion auf eine Frage oder Aussage ankreuzen.*

a) Good idea.

b) You're welcome. *(Bitte./Gern geschehen.)*

c) Fine, thanks.

C Reading

Allgemeiner Hinweis: *In diesem Prüfungsteil darfst du ein zweisprachiges Wörterbuch benutzen.*

Aufgabe 1

lines 1–10	lines 11–25	lines 26–37	lines 38–46	lines 47–58	lines 59–69	lines 70–81
D	H	A	C	B	F	G

Aufgabe 2

Hinweis: *Markiere im Text die Sätze, die das Gleiche bedeuten wie die angegebenen Sätze, und schreibe sie auf.*

a) A movie has been made about him.
   Hinweis: *Z. 7 f*

b) (Today) around 700 million people have Facebook accounts.
   oder: (He started) a company that millions of people all over the world use.
   Hinweis: *Z. 26 f. und Z. 5 ff.*

c) You can contact individuals and groups easily.
   Hinweis: *Z. 39 f.*

d) Of course there are some users who aren't worried about protecting their data.
oder:
They don't mind if everyone can see them and read about them.
Hinweis: *Z. 62 ff. und S. Z. 64 ff.*

Aufgabe 3

Hinweis: *Lies den Text noch einmal durch und beantworte die Fragen in Stichpunkten oder kurzen Sätzen.*

a) (near) New York (City)
   Hinweis: *Z. 15 f.*

b) ZuckNet
   Hinweis: *Z. 19*

c) in 2003
   Hinweis: *Z. 22*

d) Facebook passes on data to other companies.
   Hinweis: *Z. 56 f.*
   oder:
   (through) advertisements/advertising
   Hinweis: *Z. 50–53*

e) telephone
   face-to-face conversation
   handwritten letter(s)
   Hinweis: *Z. 75 ff. (Im Text sind drei Möglichkeiten erwähnt, von denen du zwei angeben musst.)*

D Text Production

Allgemeiner Hinweis: *Auch in diesem Prüfungsteil darfst du ein zweisprachiges Wörterbuch verwenden. Entscheide dich bei der Bearbeitung entweder für die E-mail oder für die Bildergeschichte.*

1. Correspondence: E-Mail

Hinweis: *In der Aufgabenstellung findest du Vorgaben zum Inhalt der E-mail. Baue alle Vorgaben in deinen Text ein. Hier und da sollst du eigene Ideen hinzufügen, z.B. über den Fundort des Handys. Da du einem Freund/einer Urlaubsbekanntschaft schreibst, kannst du Umgangssprache verwenden.*

Hi Luca,

How are you? I hope you are fine. My family and I returned from Italy yesterday. Guess what I found on the day you left: your mobile phone! When I went to the beach I saw it on the bench that we had sat on. I could send you the mobile by post. Is that OK with you or do you have another idea?

I'm sorry that you had to go home one week before I did. It was pretty boring after that. How was your trip home? I hope you had a good journey.

After you left I spent most of the time with my family. We visited some of the nearby towns and went shopping. I also went jogging every day.

I attached the photos I took on your last day. I think they are quite funny. Please also send me the photos that you have taken.

I hope to hear from you soon!

Bye,

Emily

2. Picture-based Writing:

Hinweis: Bevor du mit dem Schreiben beginnst, solltest du die Abbildungen genau betrachten. Verwende die inhaltlichen Vorgaben, die du in den Sprechblasen findest, in deinem Text und arbeite den Hauptteil sowie das Ende der Geschichte aus.

… Anna was trying on the dress when Julia suddenly saw a wallet. It was under the bench of the changing room. Julia looked inside the wallet and found a card with the name "David Brown" on it and a mobile phone number. At the same time Anna saw the price tag of the dress. It cost 99 pounds! Anna didn't have so much money. So she had to put back the dress. Anna looked at other dresses that cost less. But she didn't like any of them. In the meantime, Julia called Mr Brown. She said: "Hello, is that Mr Brown? I found your wallet!" He was very happy and answered: "Let's meet at the café at 3 pm." When Anna and Julia met Mr Brown to give him his wallet, he gave each girl 20 pounds. The girls were very excited. Julia lent[1] Anna her 20 pounds. With the extra money Anna could buy the nice dress after all.

1 to lend: (ver)leihen

Notenschlüssel

Notenstufen	1	2	3	4	5	6
Punkte	72–64	63,5–52	51,5–39	38,5–25	24,5–12	11,5–0

A Listening

Allgemeiner Hinweis: *Die Hörtexte werden in der Prüfung auf CD dargeboten. Die Aufnahmen werden insgesamt zweimal ohne zusätzliche Erklärungen oder Unterbrechungen abgespielt. Lies dir die Aufgaben vor dem Hören genau durch. Während des Hörens, bzw. im Anschluss daran, bearbeitest du die zugehörigen Aufgaben. Bei den Aufgaben (Tasks) 1 und 3 darfst du jeweils nur <u>ein</u> Kästchen pro Reihe ankreuzen. Markierst du mehrere Kästchen, bekommst du keinen Punkt für die jeweilige Teilaufgabe.*

Part 1

RECEPTIONIST: Hi, can I help you?
PAUL: Hi, yeah, we wanted to know if we can book a boat trip.
ALISON: And maybe you could recommend one to us.
RECEPTIONIST: Sure. A lot of our guests do this one. *(Gets a brochure and opens it.)*
5 ALISON: Oh, dolphins!
RECEPTIONIST: Yeah. This is a four-hour trip to watch the wild dolphins and their babies.
PAUL: Great, and can we go in the water, too?
RECEPTIONIST: Yeah, you can go snorkeling but not where the dolphins are, of
10 course.
PAUL: Yeah, OK. And are there trips every day?
RECEPTIONIST: Yeah, every day, leaving at 9 o'clock and getting back at around 1.30.
ALISON: OK. And how much does it cost?
15 RECEPTIONIST: Well, it's usually $ 95 over the phone and 90 over the internet, but we can do it for you for 85.
PAUL: OK.
ALISON: And do we have to book in advance?
RECEPTIONIST: You do, I'm afraid. The day before. Tomorrow's trip is almost full
20 but there's still space on Friday.
PAUL: OK, we'll think about it and let you know.

Vokabelhinweise:

Z. 3: to recommend: empfehlen
Z. 9: to snorkel: schnorcheln
Z. 18: in advance: im Voraus

1. watch dolphins.
   / Hinweis: *Z. 6 f.*

2. snorkeling.
   / Hinweis: *Z. 9*

3. 9 to 1.30.
   / Hinweis: *Z. 12 f.*

4. $ 85.
   / Hinweis: *Z. 16*

5. on Friday.
   / Hinweis: *Z. 20*

Part 2

1 TV MAN: OK, and let's have a look at the weather coming up over the next three
days. Today it's going to be partly cloudy with temperatures steady at around
75 Fahrenheit. The chance of rain is about 20 % and the easterly winds are
going to be between 15 to 20 mph.

5 Tomorrow, Thursday, it's going to feel quite breezy, too, with easterly winds
between 25 to 30 mph. There's going to be a mix of sunshine and clouds. The
chance of rain will be around 30 %, but all in all it'll feel warm out there with
temperatures reaching a high of 85.

Moving on to Friday now. Friday's going to start clear and bright but with

10 easterly winds reaching 35 mph there's a 50 % chance of rain by the late afternoon. Temperatures are going to climb to a maximum of 95 and it's going to
feel pretty humid, too.

OK, so after the break, we'll be welcoming a special guest because *(fade begins
here)* City Manager Billy Wardlow will be here to talk about the new parking

15 regulations that are being introduced next year and what they're going to mean.

Vokabelhinweise:
Z. 2: partly cloudy: teilweise bewölkt; steady: gleichbleibend (konstant)
Z. 5: breezy: windig

	Temperature in Fahrenheit (°F)	Chance of rain in percent (%)	Winds in miles per hour (mph)
Today	75	20	15–20
Thursday	85	30	25–30
Friday	95	50	35

Hinweis: *In den USA wird v. a. die Fahrenheit-Skala verwendet, um Temperaturen anzugeben: 75° Fahrenheit (Z. 3) = 23,9 °C, 85° Fahrenheit (Z. 8) = 29,4 °C, 95° Fahrenheit (Z. 11) = 35 °C.*

In einigen englischsprachigen Ländern wird die Einheit mph (miles per hour) verwendet, um Geschwindigkeiten anzugeben: 35 mph (Z. 10) entsprechen rund 56 km/h.

Die richtigen Lösungen findest du in folgenden Abschnitten: Today (Z. 2–4), Thursday (Z. 5–8), Friday (Z. 9–12)

Part 3

RECEPTIONIST: Hello there.
PAUL/ALISON: Hi.
RECEPTIONIST: Made up your mind about the boat trip yet?
PAUL: Yeah, we'd like to book for tomorrow if that's possible.
RECEPTIONIST: Oh, I'm sorry but tomorrow's trip's been cancelled because of the bad weather. How about Saturday?
ALISON: We're leaving on Saturday. Tomorrow's our last day.
RECEPTIONIST: Have you thought about going to *SeaWorld*?
PAUL: But that's quite a long way, isn't it?
RECEPTIONIST: Yeah, you're right, about 140 miles, so about 2 hours by car.
ALISON: Do you really want to be sitting in a car for four hours if we've got a 10-hour flight the next day?
PAUL: No, you're right.
ALISON: I'd rather be here tomorrow.
PAUL: And today? What else could we do?
RECEPTIONIST: Have you ever tried parasailing – you know, in a parachute from behind a boat?
ALISON: That sounds cool!
RECEPTIONIST: You can do it together – tandem parasailing.
PAUL: Locally?
RECEPTIONIST: Yes, there's a place about ten minutes on foot from here. I'll show you on the map where it is.
ALISON: Great. Then we can walk down there and check it out.
PAUL: That's a good idea.

Vokabelhinweise:

Z. 10: 140 miles: ca. 225 km
Z. 16: parachute: Fallschirm
Z. 20: locally: in der Nähe

1. False
   Hinweis: Z. 5 (*"tomorrow's trip's been cancelled"*)
2. True
   Hinweis: Z. 7
3. False
   Hinweis: Z. 10
4. True
   Hinweis: Z. 19
5. False
   Hinweis: Z. 21 (*"on foot"*)

Part 4

1 SUNRISE: Hi, how can I help?
ALISON: Hi, I wanted to ask if we can join one of your trips today.
SUNRISE: Sure. When do you want to go?
ALISON: Well, this afternoon would be great.
5 SUNRISE: How about 2 o'clock. Or 3 o'clock?
ALISON: Two's fine. Do we need to bring anything special with us?
SUNRISE: Well the usual stuff – a towel, sunscreen and sunglasses. Oh, and your
   camera, of course.
ALISON: And do you need to see our passports?
10 SUNRISE: No, no.
ALISON: No identification or anything?
SUNRISE: No, just the name of the hotel where you're staying.
ALISON: OK. Um … oh yes: my boyfriend's a bit scared of heights so I wanted to
   know how high up we go.
15 SUNRISE: About 500 feet – but that's the maximum.
ALISON: Okay. And how long is the trip?
SUNRISE: About 45 minutes, and you're up in the air for about 10 minutes. But
   your boyfriend needn't worry. You'll be up there with him holding his hand!
Alison: True. I'll tell him that.

Vokabelhinweise:
Z. 7: sunscreen: Sonnencreme
Z. 11: identification: Ausweis
Z. 15: 500 feet: ca. 153 m

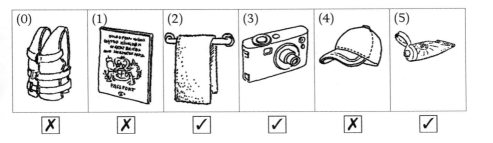

B Use of English

Hinweis: *In diesem Teil werden dein Wortschatz und deine Grammatik-Kenntnisse geprüft. Sind bei einer Aufgabe Wörter bereits vorgegeben, achte beim Einsetzen des ausgewählten Wortes in die Lücke darauf, das Wort richtig zu schreiben. Abschreibfehler führen nämlich zu Punktverlust, den du mit etwas Sorgfalt vermeiden kannst.*

Aufgabe 1

Hinweis: *Setze hier die passenden Wörter ein. Überlege dir, wie die einzelnen Wörter auf Deutsch heißen, denn einige dieser Namenwörter kann man auf Englisch leicht verwechseln, z. B. cloths (Tücher/Lappen) – clothes (Kleidung), counties (Grafschaften/Bezirke) – countries (Länder). Die schräg gedruckten Wörter im Text geben dir den Hinweis auf das fehlende Wort.*

Last year I travelled around the world for three <u>months</u> in *June, July and August*. I went to *Japan, India, the USA* and a lot of other <u>countries</u>. Of all the cities I saw I like New York best. When I was there I visited *the Empire State Building, the Statue of Liberty, Times Square* and many other well-known <u>sights</u>. I went to a fashion store and bought a *jacket, trousers, a shirt* and other <u>clothes</u> which are cheaper than in England. New York was full of tourists. I heard them speak *French, Chinese, Russian* and many other <u>languages</u>.

Aufgabe 2

Hinweis: *Hier musst du Wörter finden, die dieselbe Bedeutung haben wie die Wörter in Klammern.*

Woman: When does the show <u>finish</u> this evening?
Man: At about 10 o'clock.
Woman <u>Maybe</u> we can have dinner somewhere afterwards.

Man:	Good idea.
Woman:	Are there any restaurants close to the theatre?
Man:	I don't think so. But we can walk somewhere.
Woman:	No, let's take / call a taxi.
Man:	OK.
Woman:	And let's book a table.

Aufgabe 3

/ **Hinweis:** *Hier geht es darum, die richtige Form des angegebenen Verbs einzusetzen.*
/ *Achte hier u. a. auf die grammatikalischen Zeiten (tenses) und die Signalwörter,*
/ *nach denen eine bestimmte Form verwendet werden muss.*

/ Signalwort	Form	Zeit	Besonderheit
/ at the age of ten	learned	simple past	–
/ when	was	simple past	–
/ good at	swimming	–	-ing-Form nach
/			„to be good at"
/ usually	wins	simple present	Mike wins
/ next year	will have, 'll have	will future	

At the age of ten I learned how to surf. When I got my own board I was so happy.
Now I'm not only good at surfing. I'm also a very good swimmer. Every weekend
my friend Mike and I meet at a lake. Often we race against each other and Mike
usually wins. At the moment I'm saving for a special course in Spain. I hope that
I 'll have / will have enough money next year.

Aufgabe 4

/ **Hinweis:** *Ergänze hier die Sätze mit den richtigen Wörtern aus dem Kasten. Achte*
/ *dabei auf den Textzusammenhang.*

Jack and his sister Tina spent a weekend in London. When they got to the station,
Jack carried his sister's suitcase because it was so heavy. They took the Under-
ground to their aunt. She lives in a small flat all by herself and she is a great cook.
Whenever she has guests, she likes to cook for them.

Aufgabe 5

Hinweis: *Hier musst du einen Dialog ergänzen. Mithilfe der vorgegebenen Antworten kannst du die fehlenden Fragen erschließen.*

Tina:	Excuse me? <u>Can you help me</u>?
Londoner:	Yes, of course.
Tina:	<u>Is there a bus</u> / <u>Is this the bus</u> / <u>Could you tell me if there is a bus</u> / <u>Do you know if there is a bus</u> to the Tower?
Londoner:	Yes, it's bus number 15.
Tina:	How long <u>does it take</u> / <u>will it take</u> / <u>will it be</u> to get there?
Londoner:	Not long. About twenty minutes.
Tina:	How <u>much is it</u> / <u>much does it cost</u> / <u>much is the ticket</u>?
Londoner:	I'm not sure but the driver will know the price.
Tina:	<u>Do you know</u> / <u>Would you tell me</u> / <u>Could you tell me</u> if there's a bus stop nearby?
Londoner:	Yes, just around the corner.
Tina:	Thank you.
Londoner:	No worries.

C Reading Comprehension

Allgemeiner Hinweis: *Lies den Text erst einmal durch, damit du weißt, wovon er handelt. Sieh dir die Aufgaben an und suche die Stellen im Text, die dir den Hinweis auf die richtige Lösung geben.*

Vokabelhinweise:

Z. 8: *to take part in: teilnehmen an*

Z. 8 f.: *state-wide surf competition: Surf-Wettbewerb mit Teilnehmern aus den einzelnen Bundesstaaten der USA*

Z. 10: *passion: Leidenschaft*

Z. 13: *15-foot tiger shark: 4,5 m langer Tigerhai*

Z. 16: *to recover: sich erholen*

Z. 17: *physically: körperlich*

Z. 17: *mentally: seelisch*

Z. 17: *attitude: Einstellung*

Z. 18: *faith: Glaube*

Z. 26: *success: Erfolg*

Z. 34: *foundation: Stiftung*

Z. 35: *non-profit: gemeinnützig, nicht auf Gewinn ausgerichtet*

Z. 35: *to support: unterstützen*

Z. 35: *survivor: Überlebende(r)*

Aufgabe 1

✎ **Hinweis:** *Finde hier zu jedem Absatz die passende Überschrift.*

paragraph 1 (lines 1–10)	paragraph 2 (lines 11–15)	paragraph 3 (lines 16–20)	paragraph 4 (lines 21–28)	paragraph 5 (lines 29–36)	paragraph 6 (lines 37–40)
E	C	D	G	A	B

Aufgabe 2

✎ **Hinweis:** *Im Lesetext über Bethany Hamilton fehlen vier Sätze. Diese sind im Text*
✎ *mit (1), (2), (3) und (4) gekennzeichnet. Die fehlenden Sätze (sowie einen weiteren,*
✎ *nicht passenden Satz) findest du in Aufgabe 2. Erschließe aus dem Zusammenhang,*
✎ *welcher Satz zu welcher Textstelle passt und trage den jeweiligen Buchstaben in die*
✎ *Tabelle ein.*
✎ *Hinweise im Text:*
✎ *(1) F: "I was more scared..." (Z. 19 f.)*
✎ *(2) A: "... surfing competitions have taken her to South America, ..." (Z. 25 f.)*
✎ *(3) C: "Bethany is not only a star in the water." (Z. 29)*
✎ *(4) D: "This is what she has to say to young people: ..." (Z. 39)*

Vokabelhinweise:
to compete with: sich messen mit, gegen jmd. antreten
successful: erfolgreich
to be hopeless: ohne Hoffnung sein

(0)	(1)	(2)	(3)	(4)
B	F	**A**	C	D

Aufgabe 3

✎ **Hinweis:** *Überprüfe hier, ob die Aussagen zum Lesetext richtig oder falsch sind.*

a) True
✎ **Hinweis:** *Z. 4 f.*

b) False
✎ **Hinweis:** *Z. 13 f.*

c) False
  Hinweis: *Z. 18 f.*

d) True
  Hinweis: *Z. 39 f.*

Aufgabe 4

a)	b)	c)	d)
line(s) 6–7	line(s) 11–12	line(s) 17–18	line(s) 29–30

Aufgabe 5

a) (in) 2005
  Hinweis: *Z. 22 f.*

b) (it's) Soul Surfer
  Hinweis: *Z. 31*

c) shark attack survivors
  oder: (other) amputees (worldwide)
  Hinweis: *Z. 35 f.*

D Text Production

Allgemeiner Hinweis: *Auch in diesem Prüfungsteil darfst du ein zweisprachiges Wörterbuch verwenden. Entscheide dich bei der Bearbeitung entweder für die E-Mail oder für die Bildergeschichte.*

---

1. Correspondence: E-Mail

Hinweis: *Berücksichtige beim Verfassen deiner E-Mail die allgemeinen Hinweise zu Umfang und Form, die in der Aufgabenstellung beschrieben sind. Verfasse eine verständliche E-Mail in ganzen Sätzen. Bringe beim Schreiben die Vorgaben zum Inhalt ein und ergänze sie, wenn du möchtest, auch durch eigene Gedanken.*

Hi Chris,

Would you like to take part in an international football (*oder AmE*: soccer) camp with me? I went to an international football camp in London last summer and it was great! I stayed there for two weeks and I was able to improve my skills a lot. It was the first time that I got training from professional trainers and I also met some football stars! Just imagine, I even shook hands with Theo Walcott and I also got some autographs!

It was also great that I was able to meet other boys and girls from all over the world. At the weekends we went sightseeing in London. We visited the Emirates stadium, went shopping and one night we went to a fantastic disco.

I am going to apply *(bewerben)* for the football camp again this year. Do you want to join me? You can find some more information on the internet: www.soccer-campsinternational.com/arsenal-soccer-camp

I'm looking forward to hearing from you soon.

Best wishes,
Angela

2. Picture-based Writing:

/ **Hinweis:** *Sieh dir die Bilder genau an, bevor du mit dem Schreiben beginnst. Be-*
/ *achte auch die Aufschriften: „Happy birthday", „remote controlled shark" (fernge-*
/ *steuerter Hai), „lifeguard" (Rettungsschwimmer), „Help!" und „Ron's pedal boat"*
/ *Berücksichtige beim Schreiben der Bildergeschichte die allgemeinen Hinweise zu*
/ *Umfang und Form, die in der Aufgabenstellung angegeben sind. Denke an Einlei-*
/ *tung, Überleitung und Schluss und verwende in deinem Text auch die wörtliche*
/ *Rede. Wie die Geschichte beginnen könnte, findest du ebenfalls auf dem Angaben-*
/ *blatt. Verfasse die Geschichte in der Zeitform* <u>simple past</u> *(Signalwort: last year).*

Shark alarm

Paul always wanted to have a remote-controlled shark. Last year, on his birthday, he finally got one as a present from his parents. He was very happy. Paul took the shark with him the next time he went to the seaside. It was a sunny and warm day and some people were out on the sea in pedal boats. "The perfect moment to try my remote-controlled shark", Paul thought. He wanted to scare the people a little by letting the shark swim around their pedal boats. It worked wonderfully! Two ladies with hats got really frightened when they saw the shark's fin *(Flosse)* going around their boat. One of them threw her arms up into the air and the other one screamed "Help!" The life guard came right away and was very angry with Paul. "Leave the beach – now! You are not allowed to come back with your shark anymore!" he shouted. Paul was disappointed that the life guard didn't see the fun of it.

Notenschlüssel

Notenstufen	1	2	3	4	5	6
Punkte	80–68	67–55	54–41	40–27	26–13	12–0

Ihre Meinung ist uns wichtig!

Ihre Anregungen sind uns immer willkommen. Bitte informieren Sie uns mit diesem Schein über Ihre Verbesserungsvorschläge!

Titel-Nr.	Seite	Vorschlag

Lernen · Wissen · Zukunft

STARK

22-VT9

Bitte ausfüllen und im frankierten Umschlag
an uns einsenden. Für Fensterkuverts geeignet.

Zutreffendes bitte ankreuzen!
Die Absenderin/der Absender ist:

☐ Lehrer/in in den Klassenstufen:

☐ Fachbetreuer/in
Fächer:

☐ Seminarlehrer/in
Fächer:

☐ Regierungsfachberater/in
Fächer:

☐ Oberstufenbetreuer/in

☐ Schulleiter/in

☐ Referendar/in, Termin 2. Staats-
examen:

☐ Leiter/in Lehrerbibliothek

☐ Leiter/in Schülerbibliothek

☐ Sekretariat

☐ Eltern

☐ Schüler/in, Klasse:

☐ Sonstiges:

Unterrichtsfächer: (Bei Lehrkräften)

STARK Verlag
Postfach 1852
85318 Freising

Kennen Sie Ihre Kundennummer?
Bitte hier eintragen.

Absender (Bitte in Druckbuchstaben!)

Name/Vorname

Straße/Nr.

PLZ/Ort/Ortsteil

Telefon privat   Geburtsjahr

E-Mail

Schule/Schulstempel (Bitte immer angeben!)

Bitte hier abtrennen ✂

Sicher durch alle Klassen!

Schülergerecht aufbereiteter Lernstoff mit anschaulichen Beispielen, abwechslungsreichen Übungen und erklärenden Lösungen. Schließt Wissenslücken, gibt <u>Sicherheit und Motivation</u> durch Erfolgserlebnisse.

(Bitte blättern Sie um)

Original-Prüfungsaufgaben und Training für die Prüfung